CAMBRIDGE CLASSICAL STUDIES

General Editors

D. L. PAGE, W. K. C. GUTHRIE, A. H. M. JONES

PLATO'S LATER
EPISTEMOLOGY

PLATO'S LATER EPISTEMOLOGY

BY

W. G. RUNCIMAN

Fellow of Trinity College, Cambridge

CAMBRIDGE

AT THE UNIVERSITY PRESS

1962

PUBLISHED BY
THE SYNDICS OF THE CAMBRIDGE UNIVERSITY PRESS

Bentley House, 200 Euston Road, London, N.W. 1
American Branch: 32 East 57th Street, New York 22, N.Y.
West African Office: P.O. Box 33, Ibadan, Nigeria

©

CAMBRIDGE UNIVERSITY PRESS

1962

Printed in Great Britain at the University Press, Cambridge
(Brooke Crutchley, University Printer)

CONTENTS

Preface   *page* vii

  I   INTRODUCTION   1

  II THE 'THEAETETUS': Logic and Knowledge   6

  III THE 'SOPHIST': Ontology and Logic   59

  IV CONCLUSION   127

Selected Bibliography   134

Index   137

PREFACE

This essay was written at Harvard University during the academic year 1958–9, and presented to my college as a fellowship dissertation in the summer of 1959. It is now published without revision, not because such revision is not needed, but because I have since then been doing work of such a different kind as to prevent my going back to carry it out. There are a number of changes and, in particular, additions which I should like to have made, but it seemed better to publish the original as it stands than to postpone indefinitely the appearance of an amended version. Several of the people mentioned in the bibliography are, in my belief, better fitted than myself to carry out the task I have attempted in this essay, but unfortunately none of them has yet done so. If the deficiencies of my own effort provoke someone to displace it, I shall feel its publication to have been justified.

The essay may be regarded as the sequel to an article of mine on 'Plato's *Parmenides*' published in *Harvard Studies in Classical Philology*, LXIV (1959), pp. 89–120. It embodies on several points a modification of views I held when writing the earlier article, but I still feel (although not very strongly) that the general contention of the earlier article may be more or less correct. The arguments of the present study, however, do not depend in any way on the acceptance of my conclusions about the second part of the *Parmenides*.

The bibliography which I have appended lists only those works which I found of direct relevance to the problems discussed. It does not purport to be exhaustive, and it does not contain general works on Plato or on Greek philosophy as a whole. Where reference is made to such works, or to works whose general thesis falls outside the scope of the present discussion, full references have been given in the footnotes. This procedure has also been followed where works of modern philosophy are cited. I should, however, like to draw the reader's attention to two articles which have appeared since this essay was written: Professor Gilbert Ryle's 'Letters and Syllables in Plato', *Philosophical Review*, LXIX (1960), pp. 431–51, and Mr J. M. E. Moravcsik's 'ΣΥΜΠΛΟΚΗ ΕΙΔΩΝ and the Genesis of ΛΟΓΟΣ', *Archiv für Geschichte der Philosophie*, XLII (1960), pp. 117–29. In addition,

I regret my omission of M. Maurice Vanhoutte's *La Méthode Onto-logique de Platon* (Louvain, 1956) which, although available at the time of writing, unfortunately escaped my fallible notice.

My great thanks are due to Mr G. E. L. Owen for his criticism, and in particular for discussion arising out of a seminar on Plato's later dialogues which he conducted at Harvard University in the spring of 1959. This indebtedness is greater than could be feasibly acknowledged in individual footnotes. My thanks are also due to Mr J. M. E. Moravcsik for discussion and correspondence, and for permission to consult an unpublished doctoral thesis on 'Meaning and Being in the *Sophist* and the *Parmenides*'; to Professor Gregory Vlastos for discussion and criticism of the first part of this essay; and to Professor Werner Jaeger for encouragement and advice. Any mistakes or omissions, however, are entirely my own. I should also like to express my thanks to the Commonwealth Fund for their support, and to the Classics Department of Harvard University for their hospitality.

Burnet's text has been followed throughout, except where noted.

W. G. R.

TRINITY COLLEGE, CAMBRIDGE
December 1960

I

INTRODUCTION

My purpose is to consider the logic and epistemology of Plato's *Theaetetus* and *Sophist*. However, my primary concern is with two particular questions. First, how far did Plato arrive at a distinction between knowledge that, knowledge how, and knowledge by acquaintance? Second, how closely did he approach a conscious formulation of the notion of truth-value? In the course of attempting to answer these questions I shall offer a general interpretation of both dialogues, although I shall not attempt to offer a solution to every one of the problems which they raise. I shall also hope to show that my conclusions may be reinforced by the consideration of other dialogues which have some bearing on the two central questions, and that it is accordingly possible to trace a discernible progress in Plato's thinking on the topics which these questions involve.

Much has recently been written on both the *Theaetetus* and the *Sophist*. No discussion, as far as I am aware, has elsewhere been put forward along precisely those lines which I propose to follow, but my own treatment will inevitably overlap at many points the work of previous commentators. I shall not attempt to deal in any systematic fashion with the work of others, but shall allow points of agreement and difference to speak as far as possible for themselves. I shall, however, assume one result of my own discussion of the *Parmenides*. My conclusions in the present study do not depend in any way upon the acceptance of my interpretation of the moral of the *Parmenides*; but I shall take it as proved that both parts of the *Parmenides* represent the formulation of what, to Plato, were serious and important philosophical difficulties and arguments.

The interpretation of any of the Platonic dialogues must involve some consideration of the order in which they were composed. I shall attempt as far as possible to avoid any arguments which must depend upon a controversial dating, but I feel I should make clear the position which I think it reasonable to assume. I do not think any justification is now needed for taking the *Parmenides, Theaetetus, Sophist, Politicus* and *Philebus* to have been composed in the order in which I have here written them. Of these, the *Philebus* is not as closely linked to the other four as they are to each other. But there is general agreement that it follows them: and I shall hope to show that analysis of certain of its arguments reinforces this conclusion yet further. However, three other dialogues which are relevant to this group cannot be as confidently assigned to a place in the general sequence.

The *Cratylus*, which the stylometrists originally assigned to a place earlier than the dialogues of the so-called 'middle period', has been argued by Max Warburg[1] on grounds both of content and style to belong to the period of the *Theaetetus*. This conclusion, however, was strongly disputed by von Arnim,[2] and has not found universal acceptance.[3] That the subject-matter of the *Cratylus* is closely relevant to that of the *Theaetetus* is indisputable. But even if it was composed at a date close to that of the *Theaetetus*, its less sophisticated treatment of its subject and its stylistic affinities with the earlier dialogues make it possible to assert with reasonable confidence that it can be placed before any of the dialogues of the critical group; and its dating relative to the *Phaedo*, *Republic* and *Symposium* does not affect the questions which will here be under discussion. Accordingly, the only assumption which I make is that it is to be dated somewhere before the *Theaetetus*; as to how much before, I do not claim to hold any confident opinion.

The *Phaedrus* is almost universally agreed to lie somewhere between the *Republic* and the *Sophist*. There are as far as I know only two arguments of any cogency whatever against this view.[4] The first is a general scepticism concerning the methods of stylometry. To this it can only be answered that the method makes no claim to infallibility, but it has yielded the most fruitful results that we have. The second is the argument that the treatment of sexual love in the dialogue renders it unlikely that Plato can have been in his fifties when he wrote

---

[1] 'Zwei Fragen zum "Kratylos"', *Neue Philol. Unters.* v (1929).

[2] 'Die sprachliche Forschung als Grundlage der Chronologie der platonischen Dialoge und der "Kratylos"', *Wien. Sitzb.* ccx (1929).

[3] It is accepted e.g. by Kirk (p. 226) and Allan (p. 272), but not by Goldschmidt (p. 33, n. 7). Ross (p. 5) regards the question as still an open one: see also Owen (1) (pp. 80, n. 3; 82, n. 1; 84, n. 3; 85, n. 6) and Cherniss (5) (p. 19, n. 18).

[4] Both arguments are adduced by M. Pohlenz, *Aus Platos Werdezeit* (Berlin, 1913), pp. 355–64.

it.[1] This is at best a highly subjective consideration, and I do not find it in the least convincing. Indeed, Ritter argues on grounds at least as valid that the dialogue can only be the work of a mature man.[2] That it is later than the *Symposium* is rendered virtually certain by the remark put into the mouth of Phaedrus at *Symp.* 177 C. But its precise position is extremely difficult to determine. Von Arnim[3] places it after both the *Parmenides* and the *Theaetetus*. Hackforth,[4] after a review of previous opinions, places it shortly before the *Theaetetus* and offers the tentative date of 370 B.C. My own view is that it should be placed between the *Parmenides* and the *Theaetetus*. In addition to those grounds which have been adduced by others, I am further inclined to this view by the interpretation of the *Parmenides* which I have offered elsewhere. This interpretation, if correct, cannot positively establish a dating for the *Phaedrus*, nor does it depend upon such a dating. But if, as I believe, the *Parmenides* marks the renunciation by Plato of the hypothetical method and paves the way for the method of diaeresis as the means of resolving difficulties within the world of Forms, then it seems reasonable that the dialogue in which this method is first expounded should be that immediately following the *Parmenides*. It may be, of course, that Plato was led by considerations arising out of the *Phaedrus* to the criticism of his earlier theory and methods to which the *Parmenides* gives expression; but my own feeling on reading both dialogues (although I do not wish to press this at all strongly) is that the first view is the more plausible. In any case, I am in agreement with Hackforth's view that the *Phaedrus* is very close in date to the *Theaetetus*.[5]

The third dialogue relevant to the group under discussion is the *Timaeus*, which until recently was assigned by universal consent to the

---

[1] It is presumably this feeling which accounts for the story preserved by Diogenes Laertius (III, 38) that the *Phaedrus* was the first of Plato's dialogues καὶ γὰρ ἔχειν μειρακιῶδές τι τὸ πρόβλημα.

[2] C. Ritter, *The Essence of Plato's Philosophy* (tr. Adam Alles, New York, 1933), pp. 133–4.

[3] H. von Arnim, *Platos Jugenddialoge und die Entstehungszeit des Phaidros* (Leipzig, 1914).

[4] Hackforth (3), p. 7.

[5] I am, of course, aware of Plato's traditional assiduity in the revision of his works (Dion. Halic. *De Comp. Verb.* 208–9, cf. Diog. Laert. III, 37). This makes it dangerous to argue from the affinity of a particular passage with a passage in a later work. But where such a passage reflects the tone of the dialogue as a whole, some inference can plausibly be drawn.

last decade of Plato's life. However, Owen has attempted to undermine the grounds upon which this conviction is based.[1] He first questions the stylometric evidence. He then argues that the *Timaeus* is behind the *Parmenides* in its treatment of paradeigmatism, behind the *Theaetetus* in its acceptance that γένεσις excludes οὐσία, behind the *Sophist* in its psychogony and its notion of negation, and behind the *Politicus* in its views on government. He also points out that it takes no account of the astronomical theory of Eudoxus. The first four of these points have been strongly disputed by Professor Cherniss.[2] Although I have argued elsewhere against Cherniss's analysis of paradeigmatism in the *Parmenides*, I agree with his conclusion that it does not necessarily require us to redate the *Timaeus*. But I am less certain whether the apparent lack of logical sophistication in the *Timaeus* as compared with the *Sophist* can be regarded as altogether explained away by Cherniss's arguments. Moreover, Owen's last two points, as I have listed them, do not seem to be dealt with by Cherniss at all. Of these, the Eudoxus argument is by far the less cogent, since even on the orthodox dating of the *Timaeus* Eudoxus may quite well have produced his theory between the writing of the *Timaeus* and *Laws* VII.[3] But the argument from the *Politicus*, although it depends at certain points on Owen's own interpretation both of the *Politicus* and of the *Laws*, does at least require to be dealt with by anyone who claims to refute his thesis. Thus although this thesis cannot be regarded as proved, and has not found universal acceptance,[4] it must be admitted to have effectively questioned the orthodox dating. On the question of γένεσις and οὐσία my own views will become clear in due course: but I shall not base these or any other arguments on the fixed acceptance of any particular dating of the *Timaeus*.

One further introductory observation may be made at this point.

---

[1] Owen (1). [2] Cherniss (4), (5) and (6).

[3] I agree with Owen that the *Timaeus* does not, as does the *Laws*, condemn the description of the planets as πλανητά and that it makes clear Plato's inability to meet his own challenge (Simplicius in *De Caelo*, p. 488.18–24; cf. pp. 492.31–493.5). I further agree that it is tempting to find an acknowledgement of Eudoxus' solution at *Laws* 821 B–822 C. But even if Eudoxus left Athens for Cnidus a year or more before his death, and even if he died as early as 356, there would still be time for his theory to have been propounded at Athens after the writing of the *Timaeus* and for the *Timaeus* to have been written after the *Politicus*.

[4] It is accepted e.g. by Gould (p. 202, n. 3), but not by Vlastos (p. 238); see also Vlastos, *P.R.* LXIII (1954), p. 335, n. 29.

My purpose in this essay is less historical than philosophical. That is to say, I am less concerned to establish whether or not a particular doctrine was Plato's own or was introduced by him from elsewhere than to try to clarify the philosophical and logical position which underlies the discussion of the problems with which the dialogues are concerned. These are in many cases problems which have been neither resolved nor by-passed by any subsequent philosopher in such a way as to secure universal or even general assent; and it is for this reason that Plato rightly remains of interest to contemporary philosophers as well as to historians of philosophy. With some of the problems with which Plato was occupied I shall not be concerned. Thus I do not propose to discuss in detail that aspect of his later dialectic which is embodied in the method of hierarchical division. On the other hand, I shall, for instance, draw attention to the importance of Socrates' 'dream' in the *Theaetetus* although it propounds a doctrine which Plato rejects. These preliminary remarks will, I hope, be adequate to make clear the general purpose behind the analysis which I am proposing to undertake; and I hope also that I shall succeed in giving grounds for the view that the *Theaetetus* and *Sophist*, of all Plato's dialogues, are those of most interest and importance to the student of contemporary philosophy.

II

THE 'THEAETETUS': LOGIC AND KNOWLEDGE

The *Theaetetus* is the account of a reported conversation between Socrates, Theaetetus and Theodorus of which the object is to arrive at a satisfactory definition of knowledge. The main dialogue opens at 143 D with an introductory conversation in which, after agreement has been reached as to the sort of definition required, Socrates likens himself to the barren midwife whose task is to bring forth and examine the offspring of his interlocutors. Three definitions of knowledge are then proposed, and each is rejected in turn. The suggestion that knowledge is perception is discussed from 151 D to 187 A. From 187 A to 201 C the suggestion is considered that knowledge is true opinion.[1] Finally, from 201 C to 210 B, the suggestion is considered that knowledge is true opinion with logos; four possible senses of 'logos' are examined, but none is found to be satisfactory. Accordingly Socrates, reverting to the image of himself as midwife, sums up (210 B–D) the aporetic conclusion of the dialogue as a whole; and the dialogue ends at 210 D with the suggestion that the participants should meet again at the same place on the following morning. The discussion at this second meeting, to which Theodorus introduces a stranger from Elea, is recounted in the *Sophist*.

The general outline of the dialogue can thus be summarized simply enough. But within the discussion of each of the proffered definitions there occur several virtual digressions which are, as we shall see, of crucial importance. The consideration of knowledge as perception involves not only a theory of perception but the consideration of the Heraclitean doctrine of flux and of the Protagorean doctrine of man as the measure of all things; and this in turn leads to a virtual monologue

---

[1] I have retained the orthodox translation of δόξα. It can, however, be found misleading since δοξάζειν can take a direct object in Greek (*Theaet.* 209 B σὲ μᾶλλον ἐδόξαζον, cf. τὰ δοξαζόμενα at *Pol.* 278 B), whereas 'I opined you' would not be said in English. This point will prove to be of some importance. ἀληθῆ δοξάζειν could perhaps be rendered 'to have a true idea'.

by Socrates lasting five Stephanus pages (172 C–177 C) in which the contrast is drawn between the philosopher and the rhetorician. The consideration of the second definition, that knowledge is true opinion, is diverted almost as soon as it starts into a discussion of the problem of error. This discussion occupies the whole of 187D–200D. Socrates, having first brought forward two arguments designed to show that error is impossible, then advances three attempts to explain it, each of which is examined and rejected. The consideration of knowledge as true opinion is then resumed, and this definition is rejected by a single brief argument running only from 200 D to 201 C. In the final section Socrates, before explicitly examining three senses of 'logos', expounds and rejects his 'dream' in which knowledge is maintained to be of combinations of simples. This passage is of great philosophical interest, and has accordingly led certain commentators to assign to it too great a prominence in the interpretation of the dialogue as a whole; but its importance is clear. It is followed by the examination of the senses of 'logos', the consequent rejection of true opinion with logos as a satisfactory definition of knowledge, and the final aporetic conclusion.

That the conclusion should be aporetic need not necessarily be found surprising. It is similar to that of the *Meno*, where Socrates appears to pretend that no satisfactory account of ἀρετή has been given (100 B). Likewise the ostensible conclusion of the *Parmenides* is one of total contradiction (166 C), although the dialectical exercise which leads to this result was proposed in order to help towards a solution of the difficulties encountered in the first part of the dialogue. In any case, a continuation of the discussion is promised; and although the *Sophist* does not offer a definition of knowledge, it does make possible a solution to the problem of error which is discussed in the middle section of the *Theaetetus*. Thus there is no initial reason against ascribing to Plato the three purposes which are suggested by a first survey of the lay-out of the dialogue: first, the rejection of the definition of knowledge either as perception, or as true opinion, or as true opinion with logos; second, a discussion of the problem of error of which a solution is to be offered in the *Sophist*; third, the reiteration of the familiar contrast between the philosopher and the rhetorician. On the analogy of the *Meno* we may perhaps expect to find Plato's solution within the dialogue itself; and if this expectation is justified, it is presumably in this discussion of the philosopher that we should look for the expression of his own view as to what knowledge is. But at a first glance this cannot be claimed to be very much more than possible; and whether it is in fact likely will depend on a more detailed analysis of the passage concerned.

Two preliminary difficulties, however, can be dealt with before proceeding to a closer examination of the text. The first of these, indeed, is a difficulty which may properly be regarded as due more to Plato's commentators than to himself. It is stated by Miss Hicken[1] as follows: 'In the last pages of the *Theaetetus* Socrates is made to present four versions of a final attempt to define knowledge, as true opinion accompanied by logos, and to reject them all; yet in earlier dialogues "ability to give account", λόγον ἔχειν or λόγον διδόναι δύνασθαι is closely associated with knowledge.' Similarly Robinson,[2] after pointing out that for Plato knowledge entails logos, goes on apparently to regard this belief as contradicted by the conclusion that true opinion plus logos is not equivalent to knowledge. Now whatever logos meant to Plato, and this will later be considered more closely,[3] the conclusion of the *Theaetetus* is only puzzling if we expect, as Hicken and Robinson appear to do, that Socrates ought to accept true opinion with logos as an adequate definition of knowledge. Whether some sense of logos can be given which will in fact yield an adequate definition is not the point. But Plato may have believed that knowledge is not to be equated with true opinion plus logos without being thereby debarred from believing, as he surely did, both that knowledge entails the ability λόγον διδόναι δύνασθαι and also that logos is a necessary means[4] to the acquisition of knowledge. It may or may not be possible to establish what Plato did think knowledge to be and what he understood logos to mean. But there is no evidence, except, perhaps, a single passage of the *Meno*, that he ever supposed the simple addition of logos to be adequate to convert true opinion into knowledge. In the *Meno* (98 A) it is stated that δόξαι ἀληθεῖς become ἐπιστῆμαι by being bound by αἰτίας λογισμός. But

---

[1] Hicken (1), p. 48.   [2] Robinson (2), p. 16.

[3] I do not, however, propose to go over all the ground covered in the recent discussion in *Mind* of logos and Forms (see Cross, Bluck (2) and Hamlyn (2)). I shall regard Cross's general thesis as adequately refuted by Bluck; that is to say, I shall take it as proved that Forms are not, as Cross maintains, 'logical predicates displayed in logoi'.

[4] The importance of logos (or logoi) as a means to knowledge is often stressed by specific contrast with the inadequacy of the senses to yield knowledge, as at *Theaet.* 186 D, cf. *Phaedo* 99 E.

δῆσαι αἰτίας λογισμῷ need not be the equivalent of λόγον διδόναι,[1] for αἰτίας λογισμός is explicitly stated to mean anamnesis. The implication is that knowledge can only be of the objects of recollection, and it is this difference which will yield the ability to give a logos based on knowledge. In any case, the *Meno* contains no exposition of the Forms as such; and even if the 'binding' can be plausibly interpreted as meaning simply a deductive proof such as is elicited from the slave, this cannot be taken as evidence for Plato's views at the time of writing the *Theaetetus*. Elsewhere in Plato's writing there is a great deal of evidence that he regarded logos both as a means to and a consequence of knowledge; that is to say, that he believed both that knowledge cannot be attained without logos and that the possession of knowledge entails the possession of logos.[2] These passages make it clear that true opinion without logos is not knowledge. But they do not entail that true opinion plus logos *is* knowledge, but only that logos is entailed by knowledge. Thus it becomes clear that there is no warrant for expecting Plato to conclude in the *Theaetetus* that logos, when added to true opinion, entails knowledge. Whether, as Cornford maintained, there is a fourth sense of logos which Plato did have in mind as performing this function, and why, if this is so, it finds no place in the dialogue, are questions to which an answer will be offered in due course. But there is no initial reason for finding the conclusion of the *Theaetetus* a puzzle simply on the grounds that logos is closely associated with knowledge at all stages of Plato's writing.

The second preliminary question which may be dealt with at this point is whether, as Robinson appears to suggest, we should rule out the supposition that Plato may have thought knowledge definable by its objects. This supposition is, of course, central to Cornford's interpretation of the *Theaetetus* which Robinson sets out to demolish. Cornford's interpretation will be considered later. But Robinson,[3] on the analogy that it is no answer to the question 'what is a gun?' to indicate what the gun is pointed at, implies that Plato would have been making a foolish mistake had he thought this. However, not only does the whole central section of the *Republic* give reason for supposing

---

[1] As is suggested (mistakenly, as I believe) by Miss Hicken (Hicken (1), p. 48, n. 4).
[2] The first point may be illustrated from among numerous passages by e.g. *Gorg.* 465 A, *Rep.* 531 E, *Symp.* 202 A, the second by e.g. *Phaedo* 76 B, *Rep.* 534 B, *Tim.* 51 E.
[3] Robinson (2), p. 18.

Plato did think this, but it can also be argued that it is not a foolish mistake to think so. The gun analogy is in any case inappropriate. As Hackforth points out in his recent defence of Cornford, guns are guns even without targets, but knowledge must always be knowledge *of* something.[1] Furthermore, a fairer analogy would in many cases have been an analogy from the senses such as Plato often uses himself. Plato is, of course, mistaken in so far as he seems actually to think of knowledge as a sort of sixth sense, that is to say, a sort of mental touching; and this is a mistake of which Robinson is right to accuse him.[2] But if, for instance, an answer is required to the question 'what is smell?', 'smell is what we have of perfume' is not an altogether unreasonable or unhelpful answer. It is not, as we shall see, the sort of answer which Socrates asks for at the outset of the dialogue. But if Plato concluded that such a criterion of discrimination as he required was not in fact attainable, it is not initially inadmissible to suppose that to delimit the objects of knowledge seemed to him to be a valid way of distinguishing knowledge from some other activity which operates upon objects of a different kind.

We may now turn to the examination of precisely how the discussion of knowledge is introduced. After his preliminary conversation with Theaetetus, Socrates admits to puzzlement about 'a certain small matter' (145 D). The statement of his problem may be quoted in full: Ἆρ' οὐ τὸ μανθάνειν ἐστὶν τὸ σοφώτερον γίγνεσθαι περὶ ὃ μανθάνει τις; — Πῶς γὰρ οὔ; —Σοφίᾳ δέ γ' οἶμαι σοφοὶ οἱ σοφοί; —Ναί.—Τοῦτο δὲ μῶν διαφέρει τι ἐπιστήμης; —Τὸ ποῖον; —Ἡ σοφία. ἢ οὐχ ἅπερ ἐπιστήμονες ταῦτα καὶ σοφοί; —Τί μήν; —Ταὐτὸν ἄρα ἐπιστήμη καὶ σοφία; —Ναί.— Τοῦτ' αὐτὸ τοίνυν ἐστὶν ὃ ἀπορῶ καὶ οὐ δύναμαι λαβεῖν ἱκανῶς παρ' ἐμαυτῷ, ἐπιστήμη ὅτι ποτὲ τυγχάνει ὄν. Thus the whole enquiry into

---

[1] Hackforth (4), p. 58. Hackforth cites (with Cornford, p. 283) Arist. *Cat.* 6b2–6, where this point is specifically made. Cf. also *Rep.* 438C–D.

[2] Indeed, it is in part because of these analogies that Plato seems to have been led to think in this way of knowledge as a sort of sense. Thus in the discussion of knowledge at *Charm.* 167–9 the question of whether we can know knowledge is considered by analogy with the senses and then the passions. We can see *a* sight, but not sight; we can love someone or something, but not love itself; we can δοξάζειν what δόξαι are of but not δόξα itself. Similarly, the metaphor of seeing which stands in English for 'understanding' rather than 'knowing' is used by Plato of direct apprehensive knowledge (for references, see Lutoslawski, p. 294; against, Cross, pp. 443–4. But see also Bluck (2), and cf. further e.g. *Phaedr.* 249D–250D). Cf. also Arist. *De An.* 427a19–21 δοκεῖ δὲ καὶ τὸ νοεῖν καὶ τὸ φρονεῖν ὥσπερ αἰσθάνεσθαί τι εἶναι (ἐν ἀμφοτέροις γὰρ τούτοις κρίνει τι ἡ ψυχὴ καὶ γνωρίζει τῶν ὄντων).

the nature of knowledge begins with the specific suggestion that knowledge is wisdom. This is a notion already familiar from the earlier dialogues; and indeed knowledge and wisdom are sometimes treated by Plato as virtual synonyms. At *Prot.* 360D ἀνδρεία is the σοφία τῶν δεινῶν καὶ μὴ δεινῶν, while it is an ἐπιστήμη a few lines later at 361 B. Similarly, Socrates at *Euthyd.* 292B says ἔδει δὲ σοφοὺς ποιεῖν καὶ ἐπιστήμης μεταδιδόναι. Clearly, however, the identification of knowledge and wisdom is inadequate as a definition of knowledge if it amounts to little if anything more than the proffering of a synonym. Socrates accordingly proceeds to ask Theaetetus what he thinks knowledge to be (146c). Theaetetus replies by giving not a definition of ἐπιστήμη but examples of ἐπιστῆμαι, such as geometry and shoemaking. Socrates objects that he asked not τίνων ἡ ἐπιστήμη οὐδὲ ὁπόσαι τινές but what knowledge itself is. To the question 'what is clay?' it is inadequate to reply 'potters' clay, and ovenmakers' clay, and brickmakers' clay'; nor will a man understand what a particular ἐπιστήμη is unless he has already understood ἐπιστήμη. The correct answer to 'what is clay?' is 'earth mixed with water' (147c). Theaetetus then offers the definition of roots and surds worked out by himself and young Socrates on the basis of Theodorus' discovery of the irrationality of $\sqrt{3}$, $\sqrt{5}$ etc. up to $\sqrt{17}$.[1] But he confesses (148B) that he cannot in the same way offer a definition of knowledge.[2] Socrates nevertheless encourages him to try; and Theaetetus, after Socrates' description of himself as midwife, offers (151c) his first specific suggestion, namely that knowledge is perception.

From this introductory exposition of the problem one important point is clear. What is under discussion is not so much (or not only) what we should call intellectual knowledge, but the knowledge how of which particular ἐπιστῆμαι are particular instances. Now of course

---

[1] Theodorus apparently first took the theory of irrationals beyond the Pythagorean discovery of the irrationality of $\sqrt{2}$. The proof of the irrationality of the diagonal of a unit square is cited by Aristotle at *An. Pr.* 41a26–7. For the proof as stated by Alexander, see Ross *ad loc.*

[2] For a more detailed discussion of this passage, see Robert S. Brumbaugh, *Plato's Mathematical Imagination* (Indiana, 1954), pp. 38–44, following Heath (*History* I, pp. 202–9: on $\sqrt{2}$ see also p. 91). On the passage in general, Brumbaugh remarks (p. 40): 'The moral of the whole dialogue is one that might well be symbolized by a theorem of incommensurability; knowledge turns out, whatever unit of comparison we employ, to be incommensurable with opinion.' See further A. Wasserstein, 'Theaetetus and the History of the Theory of Numbers', *C.Q.* n.s. VIII (1958), pp. 165–79.

these two are not always, or not necessarily, so very far apart. Thus the skilled geometer is skilled by virtue of his possession of intellectual knowledge which underlies his techniques; and if, through some lucky accident of miscalculation, he were to arrive at correct results although in ignorance of the correct method, we should deny his claim to competence. But what about the shoemaker? As Professor Ryle[1] has convincingly shown, there are many cases in which people who do things well could not possibly list the facts by knowledge of which they are enabled to do so; and it is not in a conscious recognition of such facts that a skilled performance consists, but in the actual manner in which the performance is carried out. For Plato, however, this is not the case.[2] Plato's ἐπιστήμη is founded by definition upon certainty, and particular ἐπιστῆμαι depend not on the skill of the performer so much as on his possession of a knowledge which is, indeed, more like knowledge by acquaintance than intellectual knowledge. Thus at *Charm.* 170B medicine and politics are taken to be knowledge of τὸ ὑγιεινόν and τὸ δίκαιον respectively. In fact, as Aristotle points out at *Eth. Nic.* 1097a11–13, the doctor does not cure his patients by looking to the abstract idea of health. But for Plato this abstract and timeless health is precisely what the science of medicine is about (*Laches* 198D–E). Similarly, at *Laches* 194E, where it is asked what sort of wisdom courage is, the answer given is that it is ἡ τῶν δεινῶν καὶ θαρραλέων ἐπιστήμη—that is to say, the brave man is good at courage because he is acquainted with the things which are the objects of the particular science of courage. In the case of the craftsman this becomes clearer still. The shuttle-maker of the *Cratylus* or the bed-maker of *Republic* x will be good at their jobs only if they can look to the Form of which they are to fashion a likeness. In English, of course, although 'knowledge' may sometimes be used to mean 'skill' (thus 'knowledge of the game' means skill at rather than knowledge about the game, and is attributed to practitioners of the game rather than to its students), the word cannot be so used in the plural. But ἐπιστήμη in the plural

---

[1] G. Ryle, *The Concept of Mind* (London, 1949), ch. II; see also *Proc. Arist. Soc.* n.s. XLVI (1946), pp. 1–16.

[2] That skill-type knowledge is the essence of Platonic (Socratic) ἐπιστήμη is the thesis advanced by Gould. However it cannot, as Vlastos shows, be pressed to the exclusion of intellectual knowledge. Gould's treatment is useful chiefly as a salutary reminder of the extent to which the notion of skill does pervade the Platonic conception of knowledge (wisdom) not only in relation to ethics.

is frequent at all stages of Plato's writing.[1] Accordingly, the request which is made by Socrates to Theaetetus is that he should τὰς πολλὰς ἐπιστήμας ἑνὶ λόγῳ προσειπεῖν (148D). This is clearly very different from asking him to give an analysis of intellectual knowledge; and we thus have good reason to beware of any initial assumption that Plato is clearly aware of a distinction between knowing that, knowing how and knowing by acquaintance.

There now follows the examination of the claim of perception to be knowledge. It is, however, somewhat involved in lay-out, and will therefore be considered not by following the sequence of the text but by taking separately the three most important topics which are discussed in it, as follows: first, the actual refutation of the claim of perception to be knowledge based on the Protagorean doctrine of man as the measure of all things; second, the treatment of the doctrine of flux; and third, the contrast of philosophy and rhetoric. All these are closely relevant to each other; and indeed Plato for his own purposes sets out to combine the doctrine which he attributes to Protagoras with that which he attributes to the Heracliteans. But comment will be made clearer by considering the three topics under separate headings.

(I) MAN THE MEASURE

The course of the refutation is complicated by sporadic counter-arguments put forward by Socrates on Protagoras' behalf. However, there appear to be six distinct arguments brought against the Protagorean thesis, apart from the argument concerning flux.

(a) The most trivial argument is that one cannot know and not know something; but if knowledge is perception, when one looks at something with one eye and not the other, one must both know it and not know it (165 B–C). This argument, described by Socrates as τὸ δεινότατον ἐρώτημα, is fairly obviously a joke.[2] In Protagoras' defence, Protagoras is made to ask why we should hesitate to say that we both know and don't know something, and Cornford takes this to be answering the δεινότατον ἐρώτημα. However, the context makes it

---

[1] E.g. *Rep.* 522C, *Soph.* 257D, *Pol.* 308C, *Phil.* 57E.

[2] That the argument is a joke is borne out by the description of the ἀνέκπληκτος ἀνήρ putting his hand over Theaetetus' eye. Presumably Plato is also joking at 152E–153A when, in introducing the doctrine of flux, he attributes it to all previous thinkers except Parmenides, including both Epicharmus and Homer (cf. 160D).

clear that it is only the memory argument which is under discussion here, for Protagoras says that even if we do hesitate to say that we both know and don't know something, there is still the argument that the notion of one single person as percipient is erroneous (166 B–C). This second argument can be relevant only to the memory argument; and it accordingly seems clear that the δεινότατον ἐρώτημα is not followed up by Plato, and is not to be taken seriously in the first place.

(b) At 163 D–164 B memory is cited as not taken account of by perception. This is answered (166 B) by saying that the memory is merely another and quite different perceptual experience. This is not in fact a very good argument, since it makes no attempt to account for our conviction that the two are connected. But Plato does not specifically refute it. This may be because he considered it trivial; but more probably he considered it dealt with in the treatment of flux.

(c) Perhaps the most important argument is that perception cannot account for our knowledge of either expediency or right (171 D–172 B); and far the longest of the counter-arguments advanced on behalf of Protagoras is concerned with this question (166 D–168 C). Objection to the Protagorean view was first made at 161 C–162 A, where Socrates asks why pigs or baboons should not be made the measure of all things. Plato's full treatment of his argument will be best considered when discussing the 'digression' of 172 C–177 C; but it is worth re-marking at this point that the possession of skills is cited by Plato as relevant. (This ties in also, as we shall see, with the next argument to be considered.) In deciding between the expedient and the inexpedient, we take the advice of the expert (178 C–179 A). But it is not stated that it is his knowledge which guides us. On the contrary, it is his δόξα (178 D1). But presumably this δόξα (although this is not stated) is reliable because it is based on the expert's ἐπιστήμη: that is to say, his skill and not his intellectual knowledge.

(d) It is also pointed out (178 A–179 B) that perception cannot account for our knowledge of the future. This ties in closely with the preceding argument; for the criterion of expediency is accurate pre-diction, and it is for this that we consult a doctor about whether some-one is going to catch a fever or a vine-dresser about whether a wine is going to turn out sweet or dry.

(e) Our knowledge *about* what we perceive and the concepts necessary to formulate this knowledge cannot be derived from perception itself (184B–186E). This is the concluding argument directed against perception. It is the same as that first raised at 163B–C, where the point is made that simply by listening to the sounds of a foreign language or looking at letters we do not know what an interpreter or a schoolmaster can tell us about them. Similarly, our notions of number or similarity or goodness are not ascertainable by perception. This is of course a perfectly good argument against the identification of perception with knowledge. However, there is an anomaly in the way in which it is presented by Plato. The conclusion is summarized (186E) by a passage in which the claim of perception is taken to be rejected not on the grounds of its limitations but on the grounds of the nature of its objects. It is stated to be not of truth, and therefore not to be knowledge, because it is not of existence. This conclusion is taken to refute the original claim made for the infallibility of perception (160C) where it was argued on behalf of Protagoras that my perception is true for me because it is of ἡ ἐμὴ οὐσία. But the refutation is not based on the fact that perceptions cannot be true or false, but only propositions about them. (For example, 'I see red' is true, even if I am colour-blind, if I am in fact seeing what I call 'red'; but it is a lie if I am in fact seeing what I call 'green'. It may actually be purple to people whose vision is sound; but this does not affect the issue.) Plato says rather that perception is not of οὐσία which knowledge is. Similarly, τὰ κοινά at 185C–E are cited to prove not that truth or falsehood (and therefore knowledge) must be propositional, but that there are some objects of knowledge which the senses cannot apprehend. Here, clearly, the knowledge in question is knowledge by acquaintance; and the word used for how the mind apprehends τὰ κοινά is ἐπισκοπεῖν (185E2). What is surprising is that the point made just before the concluding summary is that our judgements (ἀναλογίσματα) about the existence and utility of our perceptions have to be learned, and knowledge does not reside in the perceptions but in our reasoning (συλλογισμός) about them (186B–D). This is, of course, true; and it amounts to a virtual statement that intellectual knowledge is propositional. But this is not, unfortunately, the point that Plato wishes to make, for he argues that knowledge must be of truth and one cannot attain truth without attaining existence. Truth and existence, in fact, are taken to entail each other; and the whole passage from 184B to 186C offers clear evidence that Plato does not distinguish between intellectual knowledge and knowledge by acquaintance.

(*f*) Before the concluding passage, an argument has already been advanced (170A–171C) which is designed to show that Protagoras' argument defeats itself. The remarks of Socrates at the conclusion of the argument (171C–D) suggest that Protagoras would have an answer; and this should perhaps be understood to mean that Plato was consciously overstating his case. But the argument as it stands overreaches itself by asserting that Protagoras, if he admits the belief of others to be true, and if these others believe his own belief false, must admit that his own belief *is* false (171B). This is unwarrantable. For Protagoras only suggests that 'true-for-X' should be substituted for 'true' in all cases; and although he must admit that his own view is false for e.g. Plato, this is entirely compatible with its continuing to be true for e.g. Protagoras. On the other hand, the argument does validly show that Protagoras, by doing away with any universal sense of 'true', prevents his belief itself from being universally true. He can, in fact, only advance it at the cost of any standard by reference to which it might be demonstrated. Thus Plato has made clear not that Protagoras is wrong, but that he can never show himself less wrong than those who disagree with him. Beyond this, it is only worth remarking the introduction of the notion of wisdom at 170A–B. It is introduced by citing the general belief that some men are wiser than others by virtue of their knowledge (οὐκ ἄλλῳ τῳ διαφέροντας ἢ τῷ εἰδέναι 170B1) for the purpose of instruction and government; and it is further agreed to be the general belief that wisdom is true thinking (ἀληθὴς διάνοια)[1] and ignorance false opinion (ψευδὴς δόξα). This looks like a notion of intellectual knowledge rather than the wisdom which is a sort of superior skill; and this notion seems to underlie the argument as a whole.

The result of these arguments is to offer an effective refutation of the Protagorean position. Indeed, so adequate is this refutation that consideration of the doctrine of flux would be quite unnecessary if Plato's purpose were simply to dispose of the suggestion that knowledge is

---

[1] At *Soph.* 263 E διάνοια is said to be simply unspoken λόγος or διάλογος within the mind as opposed to articulated speech. But by this time, as we shall see, Plato had come much closer to a conscious formulation of the notion of propositional intellectual knowledge. On *Theaet.* 189E–190A, see below, p. 34.

perception. This suggestion can be shown invalid whether the sensible world is in a state of flux or not. What follows from the assumption of flux is rather that knowledge is not possible at all; and it is this somewhat different contention that Plato now sets out to refute. However, examination of the arguments against Protagoras has yielded two results. We have seen that Plato has given valid grounds for rejecting the equation of perception and knowledge. But we have also seen that the lay-out and content of these arguments give evidence that at the time of writing the *Theaetetus* Plato had made no clear distinction between the three kinds of knowledge we are considering.

(ii) FLUX

The doctrine that everything is in a constant state of change is first introduced at 152D when it is humourously attributed to all previous thinkers except Parmenides. Although here and at 160D Heraclitus is cited by Plato, it is clear that he is expounding an extreme version of the doctrine for his own purposes.[1] The thesis to which the ῥέοντες (181A) are eventually driven is that everything is constantly undergoing both spatial movement and qualitative change (182A πάντα δὴ πᾶσαν κίνησιν ἀεὶ κινεῖται);[2] and it is this thesis which is the basis of the discussion. However, Socrates has advanced at 156A–157C an account of sense-perception which is introduced at 155D as offering an explanation of certain paradoxes expounded from 154B to 155C. These passages require comment before considering Plato's treatment of flux.

The paradoxes,[3] which deal with the possession of relative and apparently contradictory predicates, serve quite naturally to introduce discussion of a doctrine of total subjectivism and relativity. Plato's

---

[1] The doctrine of flux is also ascribed to Heraclitus at *Crat.* 401D, 402A, 440E (cf. Arist. *Met.* 987a32–4 and elsewhere). But on Plato's distortion of the views in fact held by Heraclitus, see G. S. Kirk, *Heraclitus: The Cosmic Fragments* (Cambridge, 1954), pp. 369–80. On the actual river-fragments of Heraclitus, see also (against Kirk) Vlastos, *A.J.P.* LXXVI (1955), pp. 338–44.

[2] Cf. Arist. *Phys.* 253b9–11. The extreme version of the doctrine is attributed to Cratylus by Aristotle at *Met.* 1010a10–15. On this question, see Kirk and Allan.

[3] Detailed examination of the paradoxes is unnecessary here. But they are somewhat oddly presented, for as Robinson observes (Robinson (3), p. 29) Plato describes three propositions as rendered contradictory to one another by the introduction of a fourth, not as being themselves inconsistent with the fourth. Against, see Cherniss, *A.J.P.* LXVIII (1947), p. 136, n. 34 citing Campbell *ad loc.*; but Plato's language is still somewhat misleading for the presentation of a logical difficulty.

own solution is not given; and Cornford and Ross both[1] attempt to find it hinted at in the exposition of the theory of sense-perception. However, the hint is that the theory will provide Protagoras' solution, not Plato's, and Cornford is mistaken, as we shall see, in holding that the theory is Plato's own. If, therefore, Plato's solution is that such paradoxes are resolved by understanding the relational nature of the attributes concerned, it is surprising to find it expounded in the course of an argument whose purpose is to establish a position of total subjectivity diametrically opposed to Plato's own. It is perhaps more likely that Plato's solution is the Theory of Forms, which is offered in the *Parmenides* as the answer to Zeno's assertion that things which are unlike cannot also be like, and *vice versa* (129 E). Similarly, the sort of paradox whereby one man can undergo different predicates and yet remain the same person is dismissed as trivial in the *Philebus* (14 C–D). Cornford, in fact, here neglects an opportunity to support his interpretation of the *Theaetetus* as a whole, for he could have argued, although he does not, that the paradoxes are an indirect recommendation of the Theory of Forms; and indeed, this could be so even if such a recommendation is not, as Cornford believes, the entire and specific purpose of the *Theaetetus*. On the other hand, the puzzles of the *Theaetetus* are more directly concerned with the relations of one thing to another, for they depend upon the fact that one thing can change (i.e. undergo a different predicate) in relation to another without actually changing itself, as when Socrates becomes smaller than Theaetetus because Theaetetus has grown. Moreover, as we shall see, Plato elsewhere ascribes doctrines to κομψοί where it is clear that some measure of agreement is implied with the doctrine concerned; and here Theaetetus remarks that he is uncertain whether or not Socrates is putting forward his own view (157 C). Thus Plato's solution may either be in the nature of relational attributes, or in the Theory of Forms, or indeed in both.[2] In any case, the paradoxes serve as a natural introduction to the view that all qualities are relative and all perceptions sub-

---

[1] Cornford, pp. 43–5; Ross, p. 102.

[2] On the general question of relative attributes, see Cornford, pp. 282–5, Cherniss (2), pp. 275–88, Ross, pp. 170–1, and Owen (2). At *Soph.* 251 B–C reference is also made to the contention that a single nominee cannot be legitimately made to undergo a number of different predicates. This contention, however, arises from the equation of identity and attribution generally ascribed to Antisthenes (Arist. *Met.* 1024 b 32, Diog. Laert. VI, 3; Goldschmidt, p. 19), which is irrelevant to the puzzles of the *Theaetetus*.

jective, so that knowledge, apart from individual impressions of sense-data, does not exist at all.

The theory of sense-perception is ascribed to certain κομψότεροι. The word occurs elsewhere of other thinkers.[1] Here, Campbell thinks Aristippus may be meant, but there is nothing in the text to suggest whom Plato had particularly in mind. In any case, all that is important for the interpretation of the discussion of flux is to determine whether Cornford is right to believe, with Jackson and Burnet,[2] that the theory is Plato's own. For this purpose it is relevant to cite the two other instances where Plato attributes particular doctrines to κομψοί. In both cases (*Pol.* 285 A, *Phil.* 53 c ff.), Plato expresses some approbation of the doctrine but withholds entire agreement.[3] This does not prove, of course, that the same applies here. But it establishes an initial likelihood which is already more cogent than Cornford's suggestion that Plato's own perception theory is attributed to others 'to preserve the dramatic properties of dialogue'.[4] This likelihood is confirmed by examination of the theory itself. For the theory states that the quality perceived is brought into being by the act of perception (156A7–B1, B7–C3, D3–6, E4–5; cf. 157A1–3); and this entails that although, presumably, objects can exist in some way without requiring the parentage of a perceptor, no object can be white, or loud, or hot, or hard unless it is being perceived to be so. A Berkeleyan position of this kind was never held by Plato, and indeed it would be incompatible with the Theory of Forms. This does not mean that Plato may not have believed the actual mechanics of perception to be somewhat as they are described here. But he certainly never thought that, for instance, the whiteness of snow did not exist unless white snow was somewhere being looked at by somebody. This extreme position, however, is a necessary part of the doctrine of total flux whereby knowledge is held to exist entirely in perception; and it must follow from this that white-

---

[1] The Pythagoreans are referred to at *Gorg.* 493 A (wrongly cited as 493 c by Campbell on *Pol.* 285 A), *Crat.* 405 D and *Pol.* 285 A. But the word does not necessarily refer to any particular school, e.g. at *Hipp. Ma.* 288 D (this I take to be the reference misprinted at Skemp, p. 173, n. 1 as 278 A) and *Lysis* 216 A.

[2] For the references to Jackson and Burnet see Cornford, p. 49, n. 1.

[3] That this is the case is less clear in the *Philebus* passage than at *Pol.* 285 A. But the conclusion of the κομψός (who becomes singular at 54 D), although it is stated that we should be grateful to him, is clearly not Plato's own since the κομψός denies not that pleasure is *the* good, but that it is good at all. For a fuller discussion of the passage, see Hackforth (1), pp. 106–8.   [4] Cornford, p. 49.

ness or any other quality cannot exist and be knowable except as and when it is perceived. Thus it is clear that the purpose of the theory of perception is to state an essential part of the notion of extreme flux which is developed by Plato for his own purpose. The arguments by which it is developed require no detailed comment. But precisely what the moral is which Plato draws from his criticism of the notion is of crucial importance.

Two interpretations are possible. The first of these, which may be regarded as the traditional interpretation, holds that Plato did believe the sensible world to be in a state of flux and therefore concluded that no knowledge is possible of it.[1] On this view, he draws the moral that knowledge must therefore be of entities beyond phenomenal flux, namely Forms. The alternative interpretation, which is that of Owen[2] and Robinson,[3] holds that such a deduction, if made by Plato, would have been in any case an error: what the argument proves is that if anything in this world were perpetually changing in all respects, then nothing could be said of it at all, not even that it was changing. Now it is, of course, true that the conclusion that we have no knowledge of the sensible world does not entail the conclusion that we do have knowledge of Forms. But this does not mean that Plato may not have thought so. On the other hand, Plato may have believed that the sensible world is in a state of flux as well as that we have knowledge of Forms without believing that the second of these conclusions follows from the first. Or he may have believed that although the sensible world is in a state of flux and our perceptions of it therefore cannot yield us knowledge, nevertheless we have knowledge of it derived by some other means. In order to attempt an answer to this problem, it will be necessary to consider the general question of Plato's attitude to the sensible world.

The concluding passage of the *Cratylus* offers a close parallel to the discussion of flux in the *Theaetetus*. Here, the moral is clearly drawn that since a nature-theory of names is not possible[4] and knowledge of

---

[1] That Plato continued to believe this doctrine, which he first acquired when young from Cratylus and the Heracliteans, is explicitly stated by Aristotle at *Met.* 987a32–b1. The question of the reliability of Aristotle's evidence is outside the scope of the present discussion; but his testimony cannot be altogether discounted. Cf. also *Met.* 1078b12–17.

[2] Owen (1), pp. 85–6.   [3] Robinson (2), pp. 9–10.

[4] Although Plato shows that if names are argued to be the exemplifications of things it can easily be demonstrated that they are in fact totally inaccurate exemplifications in

something cannot be acquired by knowledge of its name, knowledge must be acquired by the direct apprehension of things in themselves; and if this is to be possible, beauty and goodness and those other realities which we believe to exist must be exempt from flux. That Plato is here arguing for the Forms is unquestioned. He does not, however, argue that the Forms must be knowable *because* the sensible world *is* in a state of flux; he argues that the Forms must exist because knowledge would otherwise be impossible, just as he argues at the conclusion of the first part of the *Parmenides* that without the Forms communication would be impossible; and knowledge would be impossible if everything were in a state of flux (440A). From this argument it need not follow that Plato thought the sensible world to be in fact in a state of total flux. For as he points out at 439D and in the *Theaetetus* (157B, 183A–B) in a world of total flux you cannot even designate anything, let alone make any statement or have any knowledge about it. What the argument of the *Cratylus* does appear to show is that Plato thought that the sensible world *would be* in a state of total flux *if the Forms did not exist*.

Study of how Plato in fact speaks of the sensible world makes clear two things: first, that he at no stage maintained that the sensible world has no reality at all; second, that he at no stage assigned to it total reality. The first of these, indeed, is fundamental to Plato's thinking long before the writing of the *Theaetetus*, for it is by means of particulars that knowledge of the Forms (or, in the *Meno*, anamnesis) is to be acquired. Aristotle's statement[1] is, on the face of it, absurd. For if Plato retained a Cratylean belief that we can have no knowledge about the sensible world, this undermines altogether the search for common characteristics which was the starting-point of the Theory of

---

very many cases (this is the point of the somewhat tedious etymologizing which occupies most of the central portion of the dialogue), nevertheless he does not accept the conclusion that names are entirely conventional, as argued by Aristotle in the *De Interpretatione*. He explicitly argues against the Protagorean position whereby our standards are subjective and conventional (385 ff.); and although the arguments which he brings against the nature-theory are in fact more cogent than those which he brings against the convention-theory, the interpretation of the dialogue originally put forward by Grote (*Plato* (London, 1888), vol. III, p. 325) is likely to be correct, namely that Plato thought an absolute standard of naming to be theoretically desirable although not existing in fact (cf. *Theaet.* 157B, 164C, 184C; *Pol.* 261E, *Rep.* 533D–E). To accept an entirely conventional criterion would be to accept νόμος at the expense of φύσις; and this remained until the end of Plato's life (cf. e.g. *Laws* 889E ff.) the attitude most antithetical to his own.

[1] Above, p. 20, n. 1.

Forms. If the sticks and stones between which I first detect some partial and rudimentary equality are totally unreal sticks and stones, and if their partial equality is a quite different equality on each of the separate occasions on which I look at them, then they are scarcely valid as evidence on which to base my conclusions about equality in the abstract. But in fact Plato explicitly ascribes existence both to the objects of perception and the objects of ratiocination (ὁ τῆς διανοίας λογισμός) at *Phaedo* 79 A, where the two are described as δύο εἴδη τῶν ὄντων, τὸ μὲν ὁρατόν, τὸ δὲ ἀιδές. This does not mean, of course, that the first are as real as the second. Thus the bed of the bed-maker (*Rep.* 597 A) is somewhat real, but not altogether (τοιοῦτον οἷον τὸ ὄν, ὂν δὲ οὔ), and somewhat faint in relation to truth (ἀμυδρόν τι τυγχάνει ὂν πρὸς ἀλήθειαν). But it is quite real enough to be talked about as well as slept on. Similarly at *Soph.* 234D the ὄντα which are learned by experience, although at first sight they might appear to be the Forms, must in context be the facts of this world, not the next, for they are learnt by practical and not intellectual experience (ὑπὸ τῶν ἐν ταῖς πράξεσιν ἔργων παραγενομένων). Nevertheless, that a certain disjunction is still maintained is clear in the *Philebus* both at 59 A–D and also at 61 D–E where there are said to be two kinds of knowledge, one of γιγνόμενα and one of κατὰ ταὐτὰ καὶ ὡσαύτως ὄντα ἀεί, of which the second is truer than the first. Even in the *Timaeus*, where the disjunction between γένεσις and οὐσία is most radically stated, there are passages which make it clear that the disjunction is not absolute (35 A, 37 A–B, 52 A–D). The conclusion is thus that although everything, for Plato, was in some sense real,[1] it continued to be true that there was also a sense in which some things were more real than others.

This gradational ontology may seem a little absurd to our more sophisticated minds. We are tempted to say that something either exists or it doesn't, and that although beds may be broken beds or badly-made beds or not really beds (because although being used as such they were made as sofas), they cannot be partially existent beds or imperfect exemplifications of bedness or beds endowed with only a small ration of reality. We may even formalize the argument and show that $(\exists x)$ (x is not really a bed) is as legitimate as $(\exists x)$ (x is a bed),

---

[1] I am aware that *Soph.* 237 C–240 C is crucial to this assertion; but I reserve discussion of this interesting and important passage until dealing with the *Sophist* itself.

whereas (∃x) (x is a bed that doesn't really exist) is absurd. But perhaps we should also cite our ordinary use of language on Plato's behalf. For we may talk, for instance, of a colour as not being a *true* red, or a distance as not being a *proper* yard, or even a policeman as not being a *real* policeman (if he turns out to be a waxwork at Madame Tussaud's). All these cases might be taken to show that some reds, or yards, or policemen can be more real than others; and such an assertion would secure Plato's unequivocal assent. But, of course, there is a single crucial difference between Plato's view and our own. For us, existence is not a predicate, and although some reds may be truer reds than others, they are no more existent than those reds which only just scrape a qualification to be designated as such. But for Plato, as we have already seen, truth entails and is entailed by existence. Further, his word for existent is the same as his word for real; and to be ὄντως ὄν (as at e.g. *Rep.* 597D, *Phaedr.* 247E) is not merely to be tautologously existent, but to be more existent than to be merely ὄν. True knowledge, moreover, can only be of what is supremely existent; and the two kinds of knowledge are explicitly contrasted at *Parm.* 134B–C, *Phaedr.* 247D–E and *Phil.* 61D–E. Aristotle's statement is therefore reasonable enough if he is referring to the ἐπιστήμη which is ἡ ἐν τῷ ὅ ἐστιν ὄν ὄντως ἐπιστήμη οὖσα. This we cannot have of the sensible world, because the sensible world is not, as are the κατὰ ταὐτὰ καὶ ὡσαύτως ὄντα ἀεί, truly stable or truly existent; and that stability characterizes what is truly real is stated in Book x of the *Laws*.[1] But the sensible world was always, for Plato, quite real enough to be named and thought about. It must, indeed, be real precisely insofar as it is the embodiment and manifestation of the Forms which endow it with its

---

[1] *Laws* 894A μεταβάλλον μὲν οὖν οὕτω καὶ μετακινούμενον γίγνεται πᾶν· ἔστιν δὲ ὄντως ὄν, ὁπόταν μένῃ, μεταβαλὸν δὲ εἰς ἄλλην ἕξιν διέφθαρται παντελῶς. This passage is cited by Owen (Owen (1), p. 85, n. 2) to show that Plato had abandoned the disjunction of γένεσις and οὐσία, and is then subsequently argued by Cherniss (Cherniss (6), p. 240, n. 44) to show the opposite. I cite it, however, merely to show that Plato continued to believe that what is changing cannot be truly real. This belief is not in contradiction with the ascription of real existence to intelligence and change itself (*Soph.* 248A–249B) or the proposal of δύναμις as a mark of reality (*Soph.* 247D–E), for the power to act on and be acted on is different from the loss of any permanent characteristic which is μεταβολὴ εἰς ἄλλην ἕξιν. Indeed, that the objects of knowledge must be exempt from this sort of change is re-asserted at *Soph.* 249B–C. It is exemption from this sort of change that I mean by 'stability', not the κίνησις of the soul described in the *Phaedrus* and the *Laws*, or the δύναμις εἴς τι ποιεῖν and εἴς τι παθεῖν which the Forms must have to be knowable at all. Plato's treatment of οὐσία in the *Sophist* will be discussed more fully later on.

sensible characteristics and without which it could not yield us even such partial knowledge as it does.

Thus the discussion of flux in the *Theaetetus* need not be interpreted either as proving the existence of Forms from the fact of phenomenal flux, or as proving the contrary of a previous belief that phenomena have no real existence, but only Forms. Indeed, it is tempting to suggest that if Plato thought the discussion proved anything about the Forms he thought that it proved their existence precisely because the sensible world is *not* in a state of total flux. Existence is ascribed to sound and colour at 185 A, and to hardness and softness at 186 B. But the point being made is that knowledge resides in our reflections about these qualities. We perceive sound and colour, hardness and softness, and all these do in fact exist. But our knowledge of their existence and their difference from each other, that is to say, our knowledge of them as abstract qualities and not simply as immediate perceptions, is attained not by the senses but by the mind. Conversely, we cannot arrive at knowledge of existence or similarity if the evidence of our senses is at the outset totally erroneous; and if the hardness of what we touch and the colour of what we see are not a real (or to some extent real) colour and hardness, our reflections about them are unlikely to be very sound or even, indeed, to have very much meaning. But the purpose of the argument as a whole is to show that perception itself is not knowledge. Indeed this is so strongly worded in the concluding passage (186 E [αἴσθησις] ᾧ [=αὐτό in the preceding line] γε φαμέν, οὐ μέτεστιν ἀληθείας ἅψασθαι · οὐδὲ γὰρ οὐσίας) as to appear to contradict what was said before. But the point is simply to reassert that perception, though it may be a means to knowledge, is not knowledge itself, and it is only knowledge which can truly apprehend existence.

From all this it is clear that Plato's purpose is not, in fact, in any sense a discussion of the Forms. Nor, as Cornford[1] contends, is it a deliberate avoidance of such a discussion in order to show how indispensable the Forms actually are; for in the first place, the point of the argument is only to disprove that knowledge is perception, and in the second, Cornford has already maintained that the Forms have been openly mentioned earlier on.[2] The notion of total flux is introduced as a part of the theory that perception is knowledge. This theory is

[1] Cornford, p. 106.
[2] Cornford, p. 83; p. 85, n. 1; p. 86, n. 1.

refuted by showing both that it stultifies itself and that we do in fact have knowledge which cannot be accounted for by equating it with perception. If our knowledge resides only in our perceptions, then we have no right to deduce any connection or relation between one perception and another. We have no right to attribute a common characteristic to anything or to designate anything by a common name, for we can have no knowledge entitling us to do this if we have no knowledge apart from each single and separate act of perception. If observer X perceives object O at time t, he cannot assert that a subsequent perception is of the same object, for the subsequent perception is of O_2 by X_2 at time $t+n$, and to trace a connection between the two is something which cannot be done by perception itself. Moreover, this view undermines itself, since if those who hold it believe that we have no knowledge but perception, they deprive themselves of the right to formulate terms in which this belief could be phrased (183 B ὡς νῦν γε πρὸς τὴν αὐτῶν ὑπόθεσιν οὐκ ἔχουσι ῥήματα, εἰ μὴ ἄρα τὸ 'οὐδ' οὐδέπως'[1] μάλιστα [δ' οὕτως] ἂν αὐτοῖς ἁρμόττοι, ἄπειρον λεγόμενον).

Perception, then, cannot be knowledge; or rather, knowledge is something more than perception. This is not a proof of the existence of Forms, since τὰ κοινά are adduced in support of the argument rather than deduced from it. But the two are, perhaps, not so very far apart. Knowledge is not perception, because we know things we cannot perceive; but also, the things which we know must be true and immutable entities if we are really to know them. This second point is more clearly stated in the *Cratylus* than the *Theaetetus* in which, as we have seen, the first point is the one which is being explicitly made. Neither argument, of course, does in fact prove the existence of Forms, for it is assumed, not demonstrated, that νοητά are exempt from the considerations which debar αἰσθητά from yielding true knowledge. No argument is offered to prove the Forms. Such arguments have been offered in the *Phaedo* and *Republic*, but are not repeated thereafter. This does not mean, however, either that Plato recanted his belief in the Forms or that his thought is characterized by the improbable degree of

---

[1] Following Cornford's suggestion (p. 100, n. 2), for as he rightly points out the 'οὐδ' οὕτως' of *W*, which is adopted by Burnet, is still insufficiently indefinite; and οὐδ' οὐδέπως would be more susceptible to alteration than the οὐ⟨κ οἱ⟩δ' ὅπως which Cornford also suggests as a possibility.

unity which some critics have attempted to find in it. There are, indeed, important modifications in his later views, but it is not in the *Theaetetus* that these modifications find expression, but in the *Sophist*. There is perhaps, in the *Theaetetus*, some modification of the χωρισμός described in the *Phaedo* and the *Republic*. Phenomena may be being conceded some greater measure of ontological respectability, and this is possibly the reflection of the final argument of the first part of the *Parmenides*, where the difficulties of a strictly dichotomous two-world ontology are clearly brought out. But the dichotomy was never absolute, either before or after the *Theaetetus*. The *Theaetetus* is concerned to examine three suggested definitions of knowledge; and the object of those passages of the dialogue which are for the moment being considered is to show that the first of these definitions, that knowledge is perception, is inadequate. This, despite certain defects or limitations in the argument, is effectively achieved.

(iii) PHILOSOPHY AND RHETORIC

The long digression from 172C to 177C is not only different in tone from the rest of the dialogue, but is virtually uninterrupted by inter-jections or comments from Theodorus, who is for the moment the respondent. It is introduced by a restatement of the Protagorean position whereby right is equated with pragmatic expediency. This view has been originally expounded at 166D–167D in the defence of Protagoras by Socrates, and it is criticized, as we have already seen, on the grounds that it involves prediction and is therefore incompatible with a theory of perception as knowledge. This, however, is a different point from the pragmatic interpretation of wisdom. Here, the position of Protagoras as stated is not to deny the existence of wisdom (166D καὶ σοφίαν καὶ σοφὸν ἄνδρα πολλοῦ δέω τὸ μὴ φάναι εἶναι), but to define wisdom not as the recognition of absolute standards but as the ability to alter people's notions of right and wrong by reference to criteria of expediency. This is a view a good deal harder to refute than the equa-tion of perception and knowledge; in fact, the equation of perception and knowledge has really nothing to do with it. But the whole discus-sion of knowledge was introduced, as we saw, by the suggestion that knowledge is wisdom. The Protagorean view of wisdom is that to which Plato until the end of his life was always most bitterly opposed;

and he here states his own position in language strongly reminiscent of the central section of the *Republic*. He does not, however, explicitly give his own views as to exactly what wisdom (or knowledge) is. It therefore remains to consider whether despite this the passage may be taken to express his own answer to the general problem of the dialogue.

No direct refutation of Protagoras' argument is attempted, although it is in fact a very good argument. Protagoras points out that food tastes bitter to a sick man when it tastes the opposite to a healthy one, but neither is the one opinion truer than the other nor the healthy man either more or less wise than the man who is sick. The wise man is the doctor who can substitute the more for the less preferred sensations. Similarly, whatever a particular state thinks just is just for as long as the state thinks it to be so; and the wise man is the man who can persuade the state to alter its notion of justice in accordance with expediency. This is in effect a good statement of the case against absolute standards. It is weakened by being stretched to include the conclusion that all opinions are true, since all opinions derive from perception, and therefore although some may be better than others, none can be truer (167 A6–B4).[1] But this, as we have already seen, is really a separate issue which is elsewhere met on its proper ground. Here, it is irrelevant to the main burden of Protagoras' contention, which is that expediency is the criterion by which wisdom is to be judged; and it is this which is repeated at the introduction of the digression (172 A).

The answer of the digression is to contrast the true philosopher and the rhetorician. The philosopher is alone the man who is truly free, who moves in a world far above that of the pettiness and dishonesty which surround him, and whose aim is to follow the divine pattern of righteousness, knowledge of which is wisdom and true virtue (176 c ἡ μὲν γὰρ τούτου γνῶσις σοφία καὶ ἀρετὴ ἀληθινή). The language is closely similar to passages written both before and after the *Theaetetus*. The notion of the philosopher as the free man is echoed at *Soph.* 253 c and again at *Laws* 875 c–d. At *Soph.* 254 A the sophist is contrasted

---

[1] The general sense of 167B1–4 is clear, although in the first part of the sentence the text is uncertain. Better sense is made by following Cornford (p. 71, n. 2) in reading πονηρᾷ (Aldina) and χρηστῇ (*W*), although the text, despite the awkwardness of χρηστὴ ἕξις as subject, is possible as it stands. However, I cannot see the necessity to follow Diels (*Frag. Vors.*[6], vol. II, p. 260), as Cornford does, in wishing to omit τὰ φαντάσματα. For φάντασμα as virtually equivalent to δόξα, see e.g. *Parm.* 166 A.

with the philosopher, who is hard to see because the eyes of the mind
of οἱ πολλοί cannot endure to look upon the divine. The description of
the small-minded rhetorician being dragged up[1] to the height at which
he must think of justice and injustice themselves recalls that of the
inhabitant of the cave being dragged up into the light of the sun
(*Rep.* 515 E–516 A). The contrast between the trivial semblances with
which the rhetorician is preoccupied and the eternal verities of the
philosopher is closely paralleled at *Phaedr.* 259 E–260 A, where the
rhetorician learns only the semblances of justice, goodness and beauty,
not the true realities. Now there is no explicit statement in the digression of the *Theaetetus* that true knowledge is only of Forms. But the
passage as a whole is too strongly reminiscent of others where this is
made clear for it to be possible to conclude that Plato could have
written it if he had recanted his earlier belief in a world of eternal and
immutable truths which only the true philosopher can apprehend.
Moreover, it is, as we have seen, explicitly stated that wisdom is knowledge of the righteousness of the divine to which it is our duty as far as
possible to assimilate ourselves; and the suggestion at the outset of the
dialogue was that knowledge is wisdom.

According to Cornford's interpretation, it is not explicitly stated that
knowledge is of Forms because the purpose of the *Theaetetus* as a whole
is a deliberate exclusion of the Forms in order to show that they are in
fact indispensable. However, this claim is initially undermined by
Cornford's further contention that there are places where the Forms are
openly mentioned. Further, we shall see that error is unexplained in
the *Theaetetus* not, as Cornford would have it, because Plato is
deliberately withholding the Forms which provide the explanation in
the *Sophist*, but because Plato did not, until writing the *Sophist*, begin
to understand the logical and ontological misconceptions which underlie
the problem as discussed in the *Theaetetus*. If, at the time of writing
the *Theaetetus*, he had understood these misconceptions, it is absurd to
suppose that he would have written what he knew to be a confused
and unsound discussion in order to highlight the virtues of a subsequent solution. The reason that the Forms are unobtrusive in the
Theaetetus is that they are not very relevant. They are irrelevant to the
discussion of error, and unnecessary to the arguments whereby the
three proposed definitions of knowledge are rejected; although τὰ

---

[1] Cf. *Theaet.* 175 B 9 ἑλκύσῃ ἄνω, *Rep.* 515 E 8 ἐξελκύσειεν εἰς τὸ τοῦ ἡλίου φῶς.

κοινά of 185 C–D and 186A are Forms, the theory does not need to be argued as such in order to establish the point at issue. Even in the digression, discussion of the theory as such is unnecessary to the purpose. Plato rejects the Protagorean doctrine of wisdom by pointing to the true world of unchanging and divine wisdom. Plato's own ontology, in fact, is assumed, not proved. He indicates it, without expounding it as such; and there is nothing surprising in this if the dialogue is addressed to an audience which is aware both of Plato's own beliefs and of his continuing retention of them. The unobtrusiveness of the Forms would be surprising if the *Theaetetus* was a recantation of them. But there is no evidence of such a recantation, in any case. It is accordingly reasonable to assume that Plato's purpose is no more than to refute the three proposed definitions of knowledge and to give a reminder, but not an exposition, of the world of unchanging truths with which the philosopher is concerned.

After the digression, Socrates returns to the criticism of Protagoras and of the doctrine of flux by arguments which have already been discussed. These are developed into the final rejection of the suggestion that knowledge is perception, and this conclusion is explicitly agreed to by both Socrates and Theaetetus at 186 E. Socrates observes that the argument has so far advanced as to show that knowledge resides in our reflections, not our perceptions (187A), and Theaetetus accordingly suggests that knowledge is true opinion (ἀληθὴς δόξα). Socrates, however, points out that this raises the question which has often puzzled him as to the explanation of what it is to hold false opinions, or have false ideas (187D τὸ δοξάζειν τινὰ ψευδῆ). The attempt to find an explanation of error is then unsuccessfully pursued until it is finally abandoned at 200D.

Socrates first advances two arguments tending to show that error is impossible. The first of these (188A–C) is that we cannot both know something and not know it, the second (188C–189B) that we cannot have an idea of what is not (τὸ μὴ ὂν δοξάζειν). The first clearly depends on a confusion of knowledge that and knowledge by acquaintance. If, for instance, someone mistakes Theaetetus for Socrates, he is not supposing that Theaetetus is identical with Socrates, but that someone who is in fact Theaetetus is Socrates. It is, of course, impossible both to be acquainted with Socrates and not be acquainted with Socrates. But it is absurd to suggest that because someone knows both Socrates and Theaetetus he is therefore disqualified from mistaking the one for the other, just as it would be absurd to suggest that someone who knows Socrates cannot falsely suppose that, for instance, Socrates is upstairs when he is in fact downstairs or that a pair of sandals belongs to Socrates when it in fact belongs to Theaetetus. The second argument, however, depends on a somewhat different confusion. It depends partly on the confusion between seeing and knowing, for the suggestion is made that just as we cannot see something that isn't there, so we cannot have an idea of something that isn't there (189 A ὁ ἄρα μὴ ὂν δοξάζων οὐδὲν δοξάζει). But it rests also on the confusion between senses of εἶναι which Plato did not distinguish until the *Sophist*. Even then, as we shall see, he did not wholly exorcise the problem, for he never realized that both true and false statements can be made about things which do not exist (for instance, 'A unicorn is a mythological animal with four legs' is true and 'A unicorn is a mythological animal with two horns' is false; the possibility of such assertions is only puzzling if you do not realize, as Plato did not, that you can say 'There is a concept of unicornhood but it is nowhere instantiated'). But at the time of writing the *Theaetetus*, Plato seems still to have been closely entangled in the old Parmenidean problem that what is not cannot be.[1] He accordingly did not see how it could be possible to assert, deny or have an idea of the non-existent; and this puzzlement gives grounds for the attempt made in the *Theaetetus* to assimilate all errors to the mistaking of one thing for another.

Plato does not, in fact, set out to show that these two initial arguments are unsound, although this would have been the sensible procedure to adopt in order to demonstrate that error is in fact possible. Instead, he attempts to give an account of what it is to make a mistake. Robinson[2] describes him as offering and rejecting three separate explanations. This analysis, however, is misleading. It is not three separate explanations that are offered, but a single explanation (the mistaking of one thing for another) which two logical models (the wax tablet and the aviary) are then put forward to support and illustrate. Neither, however, is adequate to the purpose, and the discussion of error is duly abandoned.

---

[1] *Soph.* 237 A (Sextus, *adv. Math.* VII, 114) Οὐ γὰρ μή ποτε τοῦτο δαμῇ, εἶναι μὴ ἐόντα. See further Kirk and Raven, *The Presocratic Philosophers* (Cambridge, 1957), pp. 269 ff.

[2] Robinson (2), p. 23.

Plato, of course, is not seriously disposed to believe that error is impossible. But he does seem genuinely concerned as to how to refute an argument to this effect. A discussion of error occurs in two earlier dialogues, the *Euthydemus* and the *Cratylus*. In the first of these, Ctesippus, in arguing with Euthydemus, who has asserted that error is impossible, replies that it is possible to speak of things as other than they are (284C ἀλλὰ τὰ ὄντα μὲν τρόπον τινὰ λέγει, οὐ μέντοι ὥς γε ἔχει). This reply would seem to involve the obvious and correct contention that error is possible as soon as denial and negation are possible. If one person can assert that three is a larger number than two and another that three is not a larger number than two, it is clear that provided both disputants are speaking the same language[1] they cannot both be speaking the truth. This consideration does not, of course, help to solve the question as to what sort of things we can or cannot make true or false statements about; for instance, it does not help us to decide what sort of statements we can make about Pegasus, or the Battle of Hastings, or the present King of France. Nor does it make it clear that even in a one-word language in which the word is not 'no' it is still perfectly possible to tell lies; for instance, if my only word is 'glug', meaning bread, I can say it as I give someone a stone. But Ctesippus' assertion does at least point the way to a valid and effective demonstration that to deny the possibility of error at all is both unnecessary and absurd. However, it is unfortunately not followed up, for Plato represents Euthydemus and Ctesippus as continuing to wrangle inconclusively with one another until the intervention of Socrates some twenty lines later (285 A ff.). The argument which Socrates then advances is neither a demonstration nor an explanation of error, but rather an attempt to reduce to absurdity the contention of the impossibility of error by showing that on this argument both wisdom and ignorance are meaningless (287A εἰ γὰρ μὴ ἁμαρτάνομεν...τίνος διδάσκαλοι ἥκετε;). This recalls the argument against Protagoras in the first part of the *Theaetetus*. But it is clear that it is not adequate as a demonstration of the possibility and nature of mistakes and that this problem was accordingly unsolved by Plato at the time of writing the *Euthydemus*.

---

[1] This initial requirement, or assumption, for the purpose of doing philosophy is made clear by Plato himself at *Charm.* 159 A and *Meno* 82 B, although he does not undertake any examination of the philosophical problems which might arise for him out of the fact of the existence of different languages.

The discussion of error in the *Cratylus* is at once more difficult and more interesting. Its affinities with the discussion of the problem in the *Theaetetus* are clear; and this gives good grounds for supporting the assumption that the *Cratylus* is at least fairly close in date to the *Theaetetus*. There are two arguments in the *Cratylus* relevant to the question of error; and in both these Plato assigns truth-value to names. In the first (385 B–C), Socrates secures from Hermogenes, the advocate of conventional naming, the admission that since falsehood is possible (i.e. a λόγος can λέγειν τὰ ὄντα ὡς οὐκ ἔστιν) therefore its parts, which are individual ὀνόματα, can be either true or false. In the second (429 B–431 C), Socrates secures from Cratylus, the advocate of natural naming, the admission that despite his contention that it is only possible to say what is, bad naming is nevertheless possible and therefore false λόγοι. In both these arguments, Plato seems to be adopting a sort of atomistic analysis of error. That is to say, to make a mistake is taken to be to perform a bad piece of naming, or to miscouple a particular name to a particular object. If, for instance, I say 'a circle is square' I am wrongly assigning 'square', which exists and which I know, to 'circle', which exists and which I know. I am not asserting τὸ μὴ ὄν εἶναι, but τὰ ὄντα ὡς οὐκ ἔστιν: and further, I am immune against a possible accusation of knowing and not knowing something. This analysis, it is clear, assimilates the ascription of proper names to the predication of attributes; thus, to say 'a circle is square' is understood as being susceptible of the same analysis as to say 'hello, Hermogenes' to Cratylus. Moreover, it confuses description and reference; and meaning becomes on this analysis no more than a set of nominata. There is no hint in any of this of a distinction between the proposition, or meaning, expressed by a statement and its nominatum, or truth-value.[1] Plato, in the *Cratylus*, regards names as not only designating

---

[1] I take this distinction from Frege's essay 'Über Sinn und Bedeutung' (tr. in Feigl and Sellars, *Readings in Philosophical Analysis* (New York, 1949), pp. 85–102). I am well aware of the dangers involved in attributing to or imposing on Plato criteria which are not stated or even implied by himself. Indeed, I should perhaps make it clear that by the ascription to Plato of an 'atomistic' analysis of error I do not wish to draw the parallel which is sometimes drawn between the *Theaetetus* and Wittgenstein's *Tractatus*, for there is nowhere in Plato the notion of 'logical shape' propounded by Wittgenstein. However, I believe that confusions in Plato's thinking can be usefully clarified by considering them in the light of more sophisticated criteria, even if these criteria are not, and could not be, expressed in Platonic Greek. Thus I believe, for instance, that it is both interesting and useful to consider the *Cratylus*, *Theaetetus* and *Sophist* in the light of Strawson's distinction between sentences and expressions and their use (P. F. Strawson, 'On Referring',

things but as teaching something about them. Thus at 428D Cratylus answers Yes to the question Διδασκαλίας ἄρα ἕνεκα τὰ ὀνόματα λέγεται; and at 388B Hermogenes agrees that a name is διδασκαλικόν. Further, the function of a name being not merely to refer to something but to say something about it, the criterion for the rightness of naming is how far it fulfils this function (428E ὀνόματος, φαμέν, ὀρθότης ἐστὶν αὕτη, ἥτις ἐνδείξεται οἷόν ἐστι τὸ πρᾶγμα: cf. 388B Ἆρ' οὐ διδάσκομέν τι ἀλλήλους καὶ τὰ πράγματα διακρίνομεν ᾗ ἔχει;, where ᾗ ἔχει makes it clear that a name is to teach us not merely what it is that it refers to, but something about what it is that it refers to). Plato does, on the analogy of a tool, distinguish between the making and the using of a name. But this distinction is largely lost sight of, and it does not lead to the realization that the criteria by which a name is to be judged should be taken from its adequacy to perform a referential, not a descriptive function.[1] The conclusion of the *Cratylus*[2] is that since names are demonstrably, if regrettably, not infallible, certain knowledge is to be acquired by the direct apprehension of stable and cognizable entities in themselves. Names, as Socrates persuaded Cratylus to agree (435D ff.), can be deceptive (436B οὐ σμικρὸς κίνδυνός ἐστιν ἐξαπατηθῆναι); and it is misnaming, as we saw, which accounts for falsehood. The burden of the problem of error is thrust upon the individual atomic components of λόγοι, the ὀνόματα of which, with ῥήματα,[3] λόγοι are a synthesis (431C). This notion of what it is we do when we make a mistake persists in the *Theaetetus*, and underlies the discussion of both the proffered models, the wax tablet and the aviary.

In the *Theaetetus*, the initial suggestion that ψευδὴς δόξα is the mistaking of one thing for another draws from Socrates the objection (190B–E) that no one has ever believed that the beautiful is ugly or that odd numbers are even or that an ox is a horse or that two is one. This is, in fact, a restatement of the argument that you cannot know and not know something, for if you know two and you know one you cannot

Mind, n.s. LIX (1950), pp. 320–44. The parallel between Socrates' 'dream' in the *Theaetetus* and Wittgenstein's *Tractatus* is in fact drawn by Wittgenstein himself in para. 42 of the *Philosophical Investigations*.

[1] See Strawson, *op. cit.* pp. 335–41.   [2] See above, p. 20, n. 4.

[3] ὄνομα and ῥῆμα do not in the *Cratylus* appear to mean 'noun' and 'verb', as they do at *Soph.* 262E ff. where this sense is explicitly defined (cf. Arist. *De Interpr.* 16a1–b25). ῥῆμα is used for 'phrase' at 399B and should perhaps be so translated here (cf. *Symp.* 198B where ὀνομάτων καὶ ῥημάτων are clearly 'words and phrases', not 'nouns and verbs'); or it may simply mean words which are not ὀνόματα.

confuse the two. It is worth remarking that at 189E–190A Socrates describes thinking as conducting an internal λόγος; but this account does not, as in the *Sophist* (263E–264B) and *Philebus* (38C–39C), form part of a satisfactory analysis of error, since instead of leading to a propositional analysis of truth and falsehood it leads only to the conclusion that the internal λόγος consists of such inadmissible statements as those cited. The move which Socrates makes to avoid his difficulty is not to consider possible relations between the terms of his internal λόγος but to offer the model of the wax tablet. In fact, an examination of the language used discloses that the confusion between knowledge that and knowledge by acquaintance, which, as we saw, gave rise to the initial statement of what is in fact an unreal problem, persists through the subsequent discussion. ἐπίστασθαι, normally used for knowledge of facts or possession of skills,[1] is at 191E used convertibly with εἰδέναι for the knowledge we have of the imprints on the wax tablet (cf. 191D). Similarly, Socrates says to Theodorus and Theaetetus at 192D μέμνημαι δὲ ὑμᾶς καὶ ἐπίσταμαι αὐτὸς ἐν ἐμαυτῷ. At 198A, in the discussion of the aviary, ἐπιστημῶν ἀρτίου τε καὶ περιττοῦ παντός, which Cornford translates 'pieces of knowledge about all the numbers, odd and even', should in fact be translated 'knowledge *of* the numbers', for at 198B it is made clear that Plato thinks of the arithmetician as knowing numbers by acquaintance (ἀριθμητικὸς γὰρ ὢν τελέως ἄλλο τι πάντας ἀριθμοὺς ἐπίσταται; πάντων γὰρ ἀριθμῶν εἰσιν αὐτῷ ἐν τῇ ψυχῇ ἐπιστῆμαι). δοξάζειν[2] is likewise used both for 'opine that' and 'conceive of', and is even used in both senses within the same sentence (190D). This draws from Cornford[3] the comment that 'this is a good example of Plato's deliberate refusal to use terms as fixed technicalities'. But unless Plato deliberately intended to confuse his readers in order to make them more grateful for the eventual solution to be propounded in the *Sophist* by invoking the Forms, it is more plausible to suggest that this is a good example of Plato's unwillingness or inability to use technical terms unambiguously.

---

[1] The only other instance that I know of in classical Greek where ἐπίστασθαι is unmistakably used of knowledge by acquaintance is Aristophanes, *Eq.* 1278 νῦν δ' Ἀρίγνωτον γὰρ οὐδεὶς ὅστις οὐκ ἐπίσταται.

[2] On the difficulty of translating δόξα and δοξάζειν I have briefly remarked already; see above, p. 6, n. 1.

[3] Cornford, p. 119, n. 2.

In this situation, the wax tablet appears to lend assistance by illu-strating (193 B 9 ff.) how an impression (e.g. of Theodorus) previously made upon the mind may be wrongly assigned to a present perception (e.g. of Theaetetus). However, objection is made to this (195 B 9 ff.) on the grounds that it fails to explain such errors as thinking that seven and five make eleven. The aviary model is accordingly produced (197 A–199 C) in order to circumvent this objection. It does so by showing that the man who thinks seven and five make eleven is not both knowing and not knowing something, but is catching hold of the wrong piece[1] of knowledge out of those that are fluttering about in the aviary. But this does not resolve the difficulty either, for, as Socrates points out in a single brief paragraph at 199 D,[2] if a man knows all the pieces of knowledge in his mind he must be failing to recognize one of them if he can produce it when he should be producing another; and if he cannot recognize it (ἀγνοεῖν) he cannot really be said to know it (γνῶναι). Theaetetus then ventures the suggestion that our minds contain pieces of ignorance as well as of knowledge (199 E). But Socrates objects (200 A–C) that this cannot deal with the question of how we can fail to distinguish a piece of knowledge from a piece of ignorance. This suggestion, in fact, entails further ἐπιστῆμαι τῶν ἐπιστημῶν καὶ ἀνεπιστημοσυνῶν. Socrates accordingly concludes (200 C–D) that they should not have tried to explain ψευδὴς δόξα before arriving at a satisfactory account of knowledge.

Before, however, considering the resumed discussion of the nature of knowledge, it will perhaps be worth while to consider the explana-tion which Plato later gives of the nature of false judgement. In the *Sophist*, as numerous commentators have pointed out, he does not consider the problem of false judgement so much as that of false statement; that is to say, he considers how someone may validly enunciate a falsehood without being logically torpedoed by Par-menides' axiom, but he does not consider what goes on in someone's mind when he comes to believe a falsehood once it has been stated.

---

[1] I agree with Cornford's translation of 199 B 1–2. Although the word 'piece' does not, of course, occur in the Greek, we cannot speak of 'having one knowledge instead of another' or of 'the knowledge' in the sense of 'the particular act of knowledge of a particular object'.

[2] Cornford (p. 136) finds that 'this objection is obscure, and the language ambiguous'. However, I hope my summary shows that the argument is in fact perfectly clear, and that there is no further ambiguity beyond the now familiar confusion of knowledge by acquaintance and knowledge that.

This question, however, is briefly considered in the *Philebus*, where it appears that Plato had now solved the problem to his satisfaction; and this consideration will serve to reinforce the conviction, if reinforcement is needed, that the *Philebus* is later in date than the *Theaetetus* and *Sophist*. The *Philebus* passage (38 c ff.) seems to suggest that it is legitimate to impute to Plato at this stage a realization that judging (to borrow a formulation from Frege[1]) 'may be viewed as a movement from a proposition to its nominatum, i.e. its truth-value'.[2] The example considered is of a man who sees an object at a distance and asks himself what it is. If it is in fact a man, he will answer his own question by saying (or, if he is alone, thinking) 'It is a man'. He may, on the other hand, mistakenly assert it to be a scarecrow.[3] But the mind is now likened not to a wax tablet or an aviary containing separate impressions or birds, but to a book in which sentences[4] are written. If, therefore, the proposition expressed by the sentence concerned corresponds to the facts (e.g. 'The object which I see beside the rock under a tree is a man') then the judgement is a true one, but if it does not then the judgement is false (e.g. 'The object which I see beside the rock under a tree is a scarecrow').[5] A further model is then suggested to illustrate the occurrence of memory or prognosis. Socrates suggests that there is a painter in our minds who enables us to picture the assertion of a state of affairs which is either in the past (39 B 9–c 1) or the future (39 c 10–e 2). The example given (40 A) is of people who imagine themselves as securing large amounts of gold. The λόγοι of this kind are what we call hopes (40 A 6–7); and on the analysis given,

---

[1] Frege, *op. cit.* p. 92.

[2] I do not mean to imply by this quotation from Frege that Plato had explicitly evolved a notion of truth-value. Whether, or to what extent, this may be so will be considered later. But I do mean to imply that he was now emancipated from the atomism which in the *Theaetetus* (and *Cratylus*) had prevented him from seeing how to explain and demonstrate the possibility and nature of mistakes.

[3] I am aware of offering what is perhaps an illegitimate mistranslation of ἄγαλμα. But 'statue' suggests something in English which would be unlikely to be a ποιμένων ἔργον, and I can think of no more general word which could be used for what is merely an ἄγαλμα rather than an ἀνδριάς. I offer 'scarecrow' as lending greater plausibility to the illustration than a more accurate translation of ἄγαλμα would do.

[4] Hackforth (1), p. 74 translates λόγους (39 A 3) as 'words'. I feel certain, however, that 'sentences' is what is meant, as is shown by the example originally given of ὡς ἔστιν ἄνθρωπος. Further, this difference is precisely what gives point to the model of the book as opposed to that of the wax tablet or the aviary.

[5] The text of 39 A is difficult, but I agree with Hackforth (p. 75, n. 1) that there is no need to follow Badham in bracketing τοῦτο τὸ πάθημα at line 4.

these will be true if the sentence of which the people concerned imagine the picture turns out to correspond with the facts, but false if it does not. The general conclusion is summarized at 40C8–D3. It is always true that whatever opinion someone holds it is a fact that he does hold that opinion; but the opinion may sometimes not correspond to the facts, whether past, present or future, and it is in this that the truth or falsehood of the opinion lies. This analysis, it is clear, is a great deal more illuminating and more sophisticated than the unsuccessful analysis proffered in the *Theaetetus*. It is imbedded in a discussion of true and false pleasures which, as we shall see later, gives grounds for holding that Plato's formulation of the concept of truth-value was still at best an imperfect one. But the passage just discussed can be confidently interpreted as providing the answer to the problem of mistaken judgement which Plato, after the discoveries of the *Sophist*, was able to formulate.

We may now return to the *Theaetetus* and to the resumed enquiry into the nature of knowledge, which was broken off by the discussion of error at 187C. The initial question is posed again by Socrates at 200D, and Theaetetus again offers the suggestion of true opinion. This suggestion is rejected by Socrates in a single brief, effective, and entirely valid argument which runs only from 201A to C. He observes that a jury, when it gives a right verdict, is holding a right opinion; but it does not have knowledge of the facts which only an eye-witness can know (περὶ ὦν ἰδόντι μόνον ἔστιν εἰδέναι). This argument unequivocally depends upon the fact that an eye-witness (on the assumption, of course, that he is not somehow deceived by his senses) does have knowledge, in some sense, of the event which he witnesses. This is at once fatal to Cornford's interpretation of the dialogue, for if the object of the dialogue is to show that knowledge is only knowledge of the Forms, it is difficult to suppose that Plato means us to conclude that an eye-witness who has seen a robbery has been thereby transported into the realm of pure philosophical contemplation. Cornford is accordingly driven to attempt to gloss over the argument by the expedient of putting 'knowledge' in this context into quotation-marks.[1] But if eye-witness knowledge is not knowledge but 'knowledge', then the argument has only proved that true opinion is not 'knowledge'; and

[1] Cornford, p. 142: 'But here the real objects of knowledge are not to be mentioned, and Socrates is only allowed his analogous contrast between the juryman's second-hand belief and the "knowledge" of the eye-witness who has seen the fact for himself.'

this will hardly do. Robinson, although well aware that the argument depends on an eye-witness being able to have knowledge, seems unwilling to attribute a similar awareness to Plato, for he expresses uncertainty as to whether this is to be construed as 'a slip or an unnoticed implication on Plato's part'.[1] But there seems in fact no good reason for supposing that Plato was not fully conscious of the force of his own argument. It effectively serves the purpose for which it was intended, and it is surely reasonable to suppose that Plato chose it because it does so. Eye-witness knowledge is not, of course, an instance of that truest and highest knowledge which, as we have already seen, Plato distinguishes from phenomenal knowledge in the *Parmenides*, *Phaedrus* and *Philebus*. But it is a perfectly good example of the sort of knowledge which can be acquired, like knowledge of the road to Larisa or of the partial equality of sticks and stones, within the ontological frontiers of the empirical world. As such, it is entirely adequate to demonstrate the difference between knowledge derived from direct experience and true opinion derived from hearsay.

A more difficult question is why Plato does not follow up the example of knowledge which he has given in order to attempt an analysis which may yield a satisfactory definition. For his example fulfils the necessary preconditions which we might ourselves lay down as the criteria which a suggested example of knowledge should fulfil. To some, at least, of contemporary philosophers, it is legitimate to assert that X knows p if three conditions are fulfilled: first, that p be true; second, that X be sure that p; third, that X have the right to be sure that p.[2] It is clear that Plato's example of eye-witness knowledge fulfils these three conditions. Moreover, it is an example from which it could be argued that true opinion is converted into knowledge by the addition of logos in precisely that sense which Plato does not subsequently consider,[3] namely the grounds for an opinion; and this sense of logos corresponds to the third condition mentioned above, that the knower should have the right to be sure.

[1] Robinson (2), p. 5.

[2] On knowing as having the right to be sure, see A. J. Ayer, *The Problem of Knowledge* (London, 1956), pp. 28–34.

[3] On Cornford's interpretation, this sense is the ἀληθὴς λόγος of the *Timaeus* (p. 142); and it is not considered by Plato because, presumably, it is available only to the knower of the Forms and these are being deliberately excluded from the discussion. See also Cornford, p. 154.

The reason why Plato does not follow the line of thought suggested by his argument will become clear from examination of Socrates' 'dream' and the discussion arising out of it. However, a reason already suggests itself if we recall the discussion at the very beginning of the dialogue. The definition of knowledge towards which the whole enquiry is directed is one which is to comprehend a great deal more than eye-witness knowledge of a phenomenal fact. In particular, it is to comprehend such particular ἐπιστῆμαι as geometry and shoemaking; and such ἐπιστῆμαι are, as we saw, a good deal more closely related in Plato's mind to direct apprehensive knowledge by acquaintance than they are to our own notion of knowledge how, or skill. Moreover, when Theaetetus offered his original suggestion that knowledge was geometry, shoemaking and so on, he was reproached by Socrates for giving an answer which is logically vicious, since to give a list as a definition is to beg the question of what the correct definition should be. The elenchus which constitutes the dialogue as a whole does not follow the pattern of the epagogic induction of the earlier dialogues. Socrates does not proceed to collect different instances of knowledge in order to determine their common characteristic. He neglects this possible line of enquiry altogether, and instead sets about eliciting by midwifery from Theaetetus a succession of tentative definitions.

It is this procedure which is duly resumed at 201 C. The example of jury and eye-witness has served its purpose of refuting the suggestion that knowledge is true opinion. Theaetetus accordingly suggests that knowledge is true opinion plus logos; and this suggestion is first considered in the form of Socrates' 'dream'. The sense which 'logos' bears here is unfortunately not made entirely clear, although this is obviously a question of crucial importance. However, it can be shown that if it here means 'grounds' it does so in too restricted a sense to yield the 'right to be sure' which we mentioned above. For logos is in the exposition of the dream itself defined as ὀνομάτων συμπλοκή; and it is clear that whatever ὀνόματα are taken to mean, the mere fact of their being joined to other ὀνόματα will not yield anything which we should be prepared to call 'grounds' in the sense of a sufficient and valid reason to convert an opinion into knowledge. What a combination of ὀνόματα can do is to make a complex capable of being known *about*; but this is a different matter altogether. It will be convenient, at this point, to anticipate the result of an examination of the text of the 'dream'. The thesis of the 'dream' is that knowledge is only possible of complexes; and complexes arise out of a weaving-together of names. It is this thesis which is refuted by Socrates in the subsequent discussion. What the refutation therefore establishes is that we do in fact have knowledge of simples. Now if we have knowledge of simples, a definition of knowledge will have to be a definition covering knowledge of simples. The suggestion that true opinion plus logos constitutes knowledge must therefore be considered for any possible sense of logos in which we can have true opinion plus logos of simples. Three senses are considered; and since we have now ruled out any sense in which logos is something which only accompanies opinion of complexes (including anything we might mean by 'grounds for a belief that p'), the three definitions offered are in fact exhaustive. The first is the trivial sense in which logos is the expression of a thought in words. The second is the enumeration of all the parts; but this is shown to assume a complexity of the object concerned, which leaves this suggestion open to a criticism similar to that of the 'dream' theory. The final sense is the essential nature which marks the object off from all other objects; but this also is rejected by an argument which will be considered in detail later on. Thus the suggestion that knowledge is true opinion plus logos has been exhausted in all possible senses of logos. There can be no reason for supposing that Plato had any fourth sense of logos up his sleeve, for if he did it is impossible to suggest what it might be. Cornford's fourth sense, which, as we have seen, is the sense of 'grounds', has already been ruled out by the rejection of the 'dream'. Accordingly the dialogue proceeds without any evasion or disingenuousness to its aporetic conclusion. It has been shown that knowledge is neither perception, nor true opinion, nor true opinion plus logos in any possible sense of logos; and that to demonstrate this was precisely Plato's purpose would appear the natural and reasonable conclusion. The philosopher's realm of the digression, therefore, cannot be attained without that extra intuition which in the *Republic* was declared to be the reward of the consummate dialectician alone.

A return, however, to the examination of the text of the 'dream' is necessary in order to establish this conclusion. For this purpose, it will be convenient to offer a translation in which no equivalent will be offered for the actual word 'logos'. The sense which it bears will become clear from the passage itself and the discussion which follows. The 'dream', which runs from 201D8 to 202C5, may be translated as follows:

I seem to have heard some people say that the basic simples (στοιχεῖα) from which we and everything else are constituted do not have logos. It is only possible to name each one by itself but without saying anything further in connection with it; we can neither say that it exists nor that it does not exist, for this is at once to attach existence or non-existence to it, and nothing must be added to it if it is to be spoken of only by itself. Thus neither 'itself' nor 'that' nor 'every' nor 'only' nor 'this'[1] nor the many other terms of this kind should be added to it. For these run about and are added to everything, being different from those things to which they are attached; but if it was possible for a simple to be expressed (λέγεσθαι) and to have an individual logos of its own, it would have to be expressed apart from all other terms. As it is, however, it is impossible for any of the basic simples to be uttered with logos. A simple has nothing but the capability to be named, since a name is the only thing it has; but just as complexes are constituted out of the weaving together of simples, so logos comes into being out of the weaving together of the names of simples. For a weaving together of names is precisely what logos is. Thus simples are without logos and unknowable, but perceptible; but combinations of them are knowable and sayable and opinable by true opinion. Therefore when someone acquires true opinion of something without logos, his mind does think truly of it, but it does not have knowledge. For a man who cannot give and receive logos is without knowledge of what he has an idea of. But when he has further obtained logos, all this becomes possible and he is in full possession of knowledge.

An examination of the sequence of the argument at once makes clear an initial difficulty, which some commentators have failed altogether to notice and none has satisfactorily dealt with. It is that the last six lines (202B8–C5) do not really follow from what has been said before. For the theory as given in the first part of the argument is that perceptible but unknowable simples become knowable and sayable and opinable by true opinion only when their names[2] become combined

---

[1] I would here accept Heindorf's τὸ 'τοῦτο'. Buttmann's τὸ 'τό' here and at 205 c may be supported, Cornford suggests (p. 143, n. 2), by *Soph.* 239A where Cornford does propose to read it for τοῦτο. But I cannot find this a sufficient reason, for τὸ 'τοῦτο' is here needed to answer to τὸ 'ἐκεῖνο' as τὸ 'μόνον' answers to τὸ 'ἕκαστον'.

[2] I have translated ὀνόματα as 'names', for although ὄνομα means both 'word' and 'name' (and, in the *Sophist*, 'noun') to Plato, this is impossible to render in translation. This fact may be in part both a cause and a symptom of Plato's confusion between description and reference, for he appears, as we have already remarked, to think of words as names and names as disguised descriptions.

in logos. Here, then, logos would appear to involve the sense of 'statement' or 'proposition'; and, as has already been pointed out, this will not yield more than an extremely restricted implication of 'grounds'. But in the last six lines logos, which has apparently just been said to make true opinion as well as knowledge possible, is taken to be what true opinion lacks in order to convert it into knowledge. Thus before 202 B 8 logos appears to mean 'statement', not 'grounds'; and after it, logos appears to mean 'grounds' and not 'statement'.

Two moves may be made to circumvent this difficulty. The first is to minimize the inferential force of οὖν at 202 B 8. This may be supported by passages in which οὖν does not bear a strictly inferential sense; but reference to Denniston,[1] although yielding examples in other authors where οὖν simply proceeds to a new stage in the argument, finds the non-inferential sense only in narrative passages of Plato (e.g. *Charm.* 154 D, *Phaedo* 61 D). Denniston does offer examples in Plato where οὖν simply emphasizes a prospective μέν but none are at the beginning of a sentence, as here. The most natural reading is certainly inferential (Cornford 'so'). In any case, this move cannot resolve the greater difficulty in the preceding line, although resolution of this greater difficulty would remove the need to minimize the inferential force of οὖν. This difficulty, as we have seen, is that logos is stated to convert simples from being merely perceptible into being both knowable and opinable by true opinion. The only way out of this difficulty is to translate the second καί of 202 B 7 as 'as well as'. The sentence will then read 'thus simples are without logos and unknowable; but combinations of them are knowable and sayable as well as opinable by true opinion'. This, indeed, is what we should expect Plato himself to believe in view of his equation of αἴσθησις and δόξα. But it is a very odd use of καί. Neither Liddell and Scott nor Denniston offer any support for it. Indeed, where the καί joining the last two units of a series bears any different sense from where the other units in the series are joined, this sense is of 'and also' or 'and even' rather than 'as well as'. If Plato meant 'as well as', the natural and unambiguous way to express this would be οὐ μόνον...ἀλλὰ καί. Moreover, if the 'dream' did mean to equate perception and true opinion, we should expect to find ἀληθεῖ δόξᾳ δοξαστάς in the first half of the sentence from which it would be understood as applicable also to the complexes in

---

[1] J. D. Denniston, *The Greek Particles*[2] (Oxford, 1954).

the second, not in the second from which it is at best unnatural to understand it as retrospectively applicable to simples also. Indeed the 'dream' emphatically asserts that a simple is no more than a nameable perceptible (202 B 1–2 οὐ γὰρ εἶναι αὐτῷ ἀλλ' ἢ ὀνομάζεσθαι μόνον); and if it equates true opinion with right naming, this equation is certainly not explicitly stated. The natural reading of 202 B 5–7 is that complexes are opinable by true opinion but that simples are not. It is in this sense that Cornford takes it, as his translation makes clear; but he seems unaware of how much of a discrepancy it creates, although he is aware that it is impossible to be clear on exactly what the 'dream' does mean by true opinion.

However, there is a more plausible answer to all this than to extort a unique and unnatural retrospective force from καί. Plato, as in the first part of the *Theaetetus*, is incorporating for his own dialectical purposes an argument drawn from elsewhere.[1] That the 'dream' did in fact derive from some other philosopher or school seems virtually certain from the language in which it is introduced and from the occurrence of the word ἐπιστητός which is nowhere used by Plato except here.[2] But the last six lines are not really a part of the exposition of the theory of the 'dream'. Read in isolation, they are merely a summary of the general suggestion that true opinion plus logos is equivalent to knowledge. Plato, in fact, is merely tying in the 'dream' with the ostensible programme of the argument. ταῦτα πάντα at 202 C 4 cannot really refer to what has just been described, for what has just been described is the process whereby logos can be brought into being and join the names of simples into knowable and opinable complexes; but it makes nonsense then to say that 'all this' is made

---

[1] The question of the origin of the 'dream' does not affect the interpretation of the argument as propounded and criticized by Plato. But see Cornford, p. 144, n. 2 and Hicken (2).

[2] It is, on the other hand, used by Aristotle (e.g. *Eth. Nic.* 1139 b 25–6 ἔτι διδακτὴ πᾶσα ἐπιστήμη δοκεῖ εἶναι, καὶ τὸ ἐπιστητὸν μαθητόν). Hamlyn (2) argues that Plato here and at 207 A ff. is making a systematic distinction between ἐπίστασθαι and its derivatives and γνῶναι and its derivatives. But this cannot be proved, for although γνῶναι is more natural for apprehensive, and ἐπίστασθαι for factual, knowledge, it is clear that in the dialogue as a whole ἐπίστασθαι, γνῶναι and εἰδέναι are too frequently used without such a distinction in mind for this line of argument to be at all safely relied on. Thus the summary of the theory at the outset (201 C–D) states that logos makes simples ἐπιστητά; but the summary after its conclusion and before its criticism (202 D 10–E 1) states that the combinations are γνωστά (τὸ δὲ τῶν συλλαβῶν γένος γνωστόν). This in itself appears to invalidate Hamlyn's contention. Cf. also 209 E–210 A τὸ γὰρ γνῶναι ἐπιστήμην που λαβεῖν ἐστιν.

possible by the addition of logos to true opinion. The statement of the 'dream' theory proper ends at 202B7; and its import is to assert that the combination of names is a necessary prerequisite of simples becoming either opinable or knowable (as opposed to merely perceptible[1] and nameable). It is precisely this point which is then attacked in the subsequent discussion (cf. 202D8–E1).

Within the statement of the theory proper, it is fairly clear what sense 'logos' must bear, although it is unfortunate that Plato does not give a specific example of what he understands the theory to maintain. The theory itself does not state (as 202B8–C5 might appear to suggest) that a simple must be resolved into a complex (or 'have an account given of it') in order to become known. This only is the case in the discussion of Hesiod's wagon at 207A ff. The 'dream' does not say that a simple becomes knowable by being explained, or defined, or translated into a complex; it says that simples become knowable when their names are combined, just as physical simples combine with others to make compounds. It is thus a combination of ὀνόματα which forms a knowable complex, on the analogy (which Socrates at 202E claims the author of the dream to have had in mind) of letters making up a syllable. This much is clear enough. But unfortunately Plato gives no example of what sort of thing he considers the 'dream' to mean by 'simples'. The original reference (201E1–2) seems to be to physical elements out of which, like Empedoclean ῥιζώματα,[2] everything else is composed; and at *Timaeus* 48B the word στοιχεῖα is used by Plato to mean physical elements. If, therefore, Plato understands the 'dream' to be saying that the combination of the names of physical elements yields a complex possessing logos and capable of being known, then the knowability of the complex resides in the possibility of its being analysed into an inventory of simples. But it seems clear that Plato means more than this; that is to say, that he is considering ὀνόματα as being in some sense logical simples, not merely the names of physical simples. For the notion of logos as an inventory of physical parts is

---

[1] Meyerhoff rightly points out that the earlier discussion of perception has shown that what is merely perceptible is not knowable. But the question he poses is an unreal one (p. 132 'Why does the criticism of the "dream" rest on the assertion that the primary, simple elements have a name but are without logos and unknowable?'). The criticism assumes this, of course, because it is precisely what the 'dream' asserts to be the case; and it is the 'dream''s assertion that knowledge is only of complexes which Socrates sets out to refute.

[2] Empedocles, fr. 6 (Aëtius I, 3, 20).

dealt with later in the discussion of Hesiod's wagon (207A ff.), and although the arguments are similar Plato clearly does not think (despite the recurrence of the letter/syllable analogy) that he is merely repeating himself. Knowledge, in the 'dream', is of a συμπλοκὴ ὀνομάτων; and although the criticism of the 'dream' establishes that a complex is no more than the sum of its parts (204A–205A), the fact that this conclusion requires to be demonstrated shows that it is not an assumption made in the 'dream'. Thus Plato appears to be understanding the 'dream' to say (wrongly) that a combination of names creates something different from names and knowable in a way that names are not.

By refuting this, Plato establishes that knowledge is not only of complexes; and in a brief coda to the main refutation (206A–B) it is explicitly agreed by Socrates and Theaetetus that simples, such as individual letters or notes in music, are in fact more readily knowable than complexes. But of course the truth is that the 'dream' is in fact quite right in a way that Plato did not realize. For the sense in which we know individual letters or notes is the sense in which a dog knows its master or a baby knows its mother; that is to say, we can recognize them. But this is very different from knowing whether something is true or false. This sort of knowledge does require combination of ὀνόματα, for it is only propositions that can be true or false; but Plato's discussion of the 'dream' makes clear his unawareness of the difference. In the *Sophist* (251D ff.), where the alphabet analogy re-appears, Plato is aware of the necessity of understanding the rules governing the combination of the components of statement in order to understand the scope and nature of statement (in particular, false statement) itself. But even here there is no evidence that Plato was led to an understanding of the propositional nature of intellectual know-ledge. As we shall later see from a study of the *Sophist* and *Philebus*, Plato solved the problem of error but not the problem of truth.

However, there still remains the question of exactly what objects or concepts Plato considered to be covered by the ὀνόματα of the 'dream'. He seems, as we have seen, to understand the 'dream' to be claiming that a combination of ὀνόματα creates something more than a list; and further, to understand it to start by an apparent reference to physical simples in order to illustrate a point of logic rather than explain a point of chemistry. But this does not yet answer the question. The case of letters and syllables which is used for the discussion or criticism of the 'dream' is stated to be the παραδείγματα used by its author in pro-pounding it. But it is not clear whether παραδείγματα, which Plato tends to use of cases illustrating co-ordinate cases,[1] here means 'example' or 'analogy'. Are individual letters themselves examples of ὀνόματα? If so, how can any ὄνομα be a simple, since it can always be broken down into letters? Or is Plato perfectly well aware that this is not the point any more than that the true statement 'Cicero has six letters' means, because it is not also true of Tully, that Tully and Cicero cannot be the same person? That is to say, does Plato think an ὄνομα is (for the purpose of the 'dream') any word which stands for a logically irreducible concept, whether a letter of the alphabet or a number or anything else? This last interpretation is a tempting one, for it imputes to the 'dream' a very interesting degree of sophistication and indeed gives grounds for the parallel claimed by certain com-mentators between the *Theaetetus* and Wittgenstein's *Tractatus*. But it ignores one major difficulty. Elements are said to be perceptible before combination, and to become knowable only after being com-bined (202 B 5–7). Thus 'elements' are explicitly confined to per-ceptible qualities or objects. Existence, we are specifically told, must not be attached to them (201 E 4; cf. 205 C 4–10); and existence is not, we already know (185 C, 186 A), a perceptible. This narrows the scope of the 'dream' very much indeed. A candidate for the legitimate status of ὄνομα would be, perhaps, 'red': Plato then presumably understands the 'dream' to be saying that 'red' is not knowable until combined into a συμπλοκή of words, or names; that is to say, until it forms part of a statement of attribution or identity. In the sense already discussed this is of course quite true. But the point of the introduction of the 'dream' is only to set up a target to be demolished. We know already that Plato believes knowledge to be possible of abstract simples. But he uses the 'dream' to set up and demolish the suggestion that simples cannot be knowable in themselves.

One last question remains to be dealt with before leaving the 'dream', namely the status which it accords to true opinion. The answer, which has already been hinted at, is that true opinion is not really relevant to the 'dream' at all. The 'dream' states how true opinion as well as knowledge becomes possible by logos. If the difference between these two lies in logos, it must lie in logos in a different sense from the sense

[1] See Robinson (3), p. 212.

which logos bears in the 'dream'. This second meaning, as already remarked, would presumably be that of 'grounds'; but this ceases to be relevant after the refutation of the 'dream'. Within the 'dream' itself, true opinion is in fact precisely the ἀληθεύειν περὶ αὐτό which is asserted at 202 C 1 to be different from knowledge by lacking logos. In the later discussion of Hesiod's wagon, this makes perfect sense. For the man with true opinion of a wagon is presumably a man who can recognize a wagon, who when he points to something and says 'that's a wagon' is in fact correct. But this is not knowing a wagon. The suggestion which is accordingly examined is that the difference lies in his lack of logos, logos meaning the ability to enumerate the parts of which the wagon is composed. This suggestion is rejected; but it was a perfectly reasonable and comprehensible suggestion to make. Within the 'dream', however, true opinion is made possible by what makes knowledge also possible, and the difference between the two is not to the point at all.

The actual refutation of the 'dream' rests upon a simple dilemma, which is in fact summarized by Socrates at the conclusion of the argument (205 D–E). Either a syllable is merely a congeries of letters, in which case it is as knowable or unknowable as its parts, or it is something else which comes into being out of the combination of parts, in which case it is a simple and therefore unknowable. As far as this goes, it is fair enough. But the interesting thing about a syllable is not merely that it arises out of a combination of letters, but that it only arises out of a certain particular combination of letters. Thus, although Σ and Ω together make a syllable, M and Ζ, for instance, do not. A syllable is in a sense merely a combination of letters, but it is a combination carried out under certain rules. Aristotle, in his discussion of the question at *Metaphysics* 1041 b 11–33, is clearly well aware of Plato's argument in the *Theaetetus*.[1] His answer is that the extra element is the cause which makes a syllable a syllable, that is to say substance, which is not an element but a principle. Aristotle, however, is talking within the framework of his own metaphysics; and his answer is perhaps less satisfactory than the one which Plato sub-

---

[1] Cf. *Met.* 992 b 18–993 a 10. Similarly, Aristotle is not worried by the problem of the aviary that a man can both know and not know something, for he explains that knowledge of the universal or premiss can co-exist with ignorance of the particular (*An. Pr.* 66 b 18–67 b 26).

sequently produces for himself. For when the letter/syllable analogy reappears in dialogues later than the *Theaetetus*, Plato has become aware of the importance of the principles of combination, and of the way in which these consist of rules about the behaviour of vowels. That the vowels are what make combination into syllables possible is stated explicitly at *Sophist* 253 A. The answer which Plato then evolves for his own problem is that a proper knowledge of letters must involve a knowledge of how they combine into syllables (*Phil.* 17A–18D). In fact, children cannot be said to know their letters until, by being taught to recognize them in different contexts, they come to know how they can combine in all contexts (*Pol.* 277E–278C). The implication in all this is that knowledge is still of simples, but that to be said really to know a simple involves the ability to know how it can or cannot combine with others.

All that the *Theaetetus* establishes, however, is that knowledge is not only of complexes; and, as we have already noticed, Plato appends a brief coda to the refutation of the 'dream' in which it is agreed that letters and musical notes are if anything more knowable than their combinations.[1] The argument then resumes the consideration of whether knowledge can be true opinion plus logos (206C ff.). From this point, it seems reasonably clear what sense 'true opinion' bears. The specific examples given are in each case objects and not propositions (a wagon at 207A ff., the sun at 208D, and Theaetetus himself at 209A ff.), and δοξάζειν continues, as earlier in the dialogue, to be used with a direct object as well as for thinking that or about something.[2] Thus 'true opinion' (or 'having a true idea of something') is presumably being able to recognize and name it correctly.[3] But this is not

---

[1] In the *Phaedrus* (270C–D) Plato outlines the procedure for considering the nature (φύσις) of any object. If it is simple (ἁπλοῦς), the way is to consider its δύναμις, that is to say its capacity to act and be acted on. If it is complex, the way is to consider like this each of its component simples. The argument is reminiscent of the *Sophist* both in its account of δύναμις and in its emphasis that the understanding of an object involves the understanding of it in relation to others. This passage thus supports the date provisionally assigned to the *Phaedrus* and may even suggest that it should be dated between the *Theaetetus* and the *Sophist*. δύναμις will be discussed more fully in dealing with the *Sophist*.

[2] Thus σὲ μᾶλλον ἐδόξαζον ἢ ἄλλον ὁντινοῦν at 209B1–2 (cf. 209C2), but ποιήσει ὀρθὰ δοξάζειν περὶ σοῦ at 209C8–9.

[3] This analysis could apply also to the 'dream' if it were possible to regard ἀληθεύειν περὶ αὐτό at 202C1 as synonymous with ἀληθῶς δοξάζειν αὐτό and to ignore ἀληθεῖ δόξῃ δοξαστάς at 201B7. The first of these is perhaps possible (thus Cornford, p. 145, whose

enough. Plato is apparently not satisfied that a man should be able to think rightly of wagons as wagons or to know whom we mean if we say 'Theaetetus' or to point at the sun if we say 'sun' to him. For this does not mean that he really knows the objects concerned any more than the jury, despite the correctness of their verdict, know what actually took place at the scene of the crime. Plato still requires a further justification; mere opinion, in fact, lacks logos. Now we saw at the very beginning of the discussion of the *Theaetetus* that for Plato the possession of knowledge always entails the possession of logos. Indeed this is reasserted in the conclusion which Plato appends to the 'dream' (202 C 2–3 τὸν γὰρ μὴ δυνάμενον δοῦναί τε καὶ δέξασθαι λόγον ἀνεπιστήμονα εἶναι περὶ τούτου). But the question here is whether the addition of logos to true opinion is adequate to constitute knowledge. Of course the man who knows a wagon will know its parts, and of course the man who knows the sun will know that it is the brightest of the heavenly bodies that go round the earth (208 D). Indeed Plato several times in his writings asserts or implies that until one knows something properly it is impossible to say anything useful about it.[1] The question, then, is whether the addition of logos to the right idea of a particular simple will yield knowledge of that simple. It is even perfectly feasible to translate 'logos' in this context as 'grounds'. But the question then becomes whether there is any sense of 'grounds' in which true opinion plus grounds of an object (not a belief) is equivalent to knowledge.

The first sense considered is simply the expression of the thought in speech. This would, of course, apply as much to propositions as to opinions of objects, but it is applicable to either. It is later described by Socrates (208 c) as 'an image, as it were, of thought in sound' (διανοίας ἐν φωνῇ ὥσπερ εἴδωλον). This suggestion is quickly and easily dismissed, for it is obviously just as applicable to false ideas as true ones. Socrates then suggests the enumeration of parts (206 E– 207 A), and offers the example of a wagon. This is not perhaps so foolish a suggestion as it might sound, for we should, for instance, agree that a garage mechanic knows a car, or a professor of Greek

translation I here followed in order to retain the possibility of ambiguity). But the second is not, for, as has already been argued, the discrepancy which it shows up between the 'dream' and the ostensible argument is only created by the way in which it is tied in with the ostensible argument.

[1] Cf. *Laches* 189 E–190 A, *Meno* 100 B, *Prot.* 360 E–361 A, *Rep.* 354 C, *Theaet.* 196 D–E.

knows Greek, or a solicitor knows the law, better than a layman. But of course this is not quite the same thing. A garage mechanic may know a lot more *about* a car than a layman, and he will be able to name parts of the car of which the layman has probably never heard; but this fact is not going to yield a definition of knowledge. For to suggest that knowledge of a wagon is a true idea of a wagon plus a knowledge of its parts is to invite a criticism similar to that brought against the 'dream'. The question is merely moved on to a different level. If knowledge of a wagon means knowledge of its parts, we still do not know what knowledge is; and the fact is that a man can list the parts of a wagon without knowing them just as he can have a true opinion of a wagon without knowing it. This criticism is illustrated by Socrates by means of the same letter/syllable analogy; and the implication is drawn that knowledge of the letters in 'Theaetetus' or 'Theodorus' must involve the knowledge of how to spell.

3   The third sense of 'logos' suggested is rejected on grounds not dissimilar to those of the second, for the argument underlying the refutation of the second—namely, that the question is merely being postponed one further stage—is here brought out more strongly. The suggestion is that knowledge of something is true opinion of it plus the ability to state the essential difference which marks it off from everything else (208 c τὸ ἔχειν τι σημεῖον εἰπεῖν ᾧ τῶν ἁπάντων διαφέρει τὸ ἐρωτηθέν). Theaetetus asks for an example, and Socrates gives the description of the sun as 'the brightest of the heavenly bodies that go round the earth' (208D). Whether Plato means this as an actual definition is not clear,[1] but he states the point of the example to be the apprehension of a unique distinguishing characteristic. The suggestion that this constitutes the difference between true opinion and knowledge is then rejected in an argument which takes Theaetetus himself as an example (209 A–210 B). The argument rests on the dilemma that either a true idea of Theaetetus must already include a knowledge of his differentness, or if it only includes a true idea of his differentness then

---

[1] If he did, it is not a very good definition, as Aristotle shows himself well aware. At *Met.* 1040 a 27–b 4 he points out that definitions can be mistaken either in adding irrelevant attributes or in giving attributes which are not peculiar to the object being defined. Thus the sun would still be the sun even if it stopped going round the earth. Plato, however, seems only to mean to give a designation which is not (for the moment, at least) applicable to any other object. Whether the sun would still be the sun if a brighter heavenly body were to appear from outer space is not really relevant to the purpose of this illustration.

the problem is still unsolved. In the first case, the suggested addition of logos will merely amount to a suggestion that we should acquire what we already have in order to learn what we already think (209 E 2–4). In the second, the answer to the question 'what is knowledge?' will be 'true opinion plus knowledge of differentness' (210 A 3–4). Accordingly the third and final suggestion of a sense of logos in which it will convert true opinion into knowledge is dismissed as inadequate (210 A). Theaetetus confesses himself unable to offer any further suggestion (210 B), and on this note the dialogue ends.

These arguments in the last part of the *Theaetetus* are perfectly sound. It is perhaps tempting to suggest that they are misguided, for there cannot be a difference between a true idea of an object and a recognitive knowledge by acquaintance of an object of the kind which there is between a jury's opinion and the knowledge of an eye-witness. But that there is no sense of logos whereby there could be such a difference is precisely what Plato set out to demonstrate. It is worth remarking that the objects which he takes for examples in the last two arguments are objects of different logical kinds; a wagon is a member of the class of wagons, but Plato appears to regard both 'Theaetetus' and 'the sun' as words (or names) having reference only to a single nominee. However, whether or not Plato was aware of the extent and nature of the difference between his examples, the fact of the difference does not impugn the validity of the arguments. Once it has been established that knowledge is not only of complexes, the suggestion that knowledge is true opinion plus logos can be refuted by citing any object for which this is demonstrably not the case. Plato's examples are in fact chosen in a way to favour the suggestions just as much as the refutations. For a wagon is something which does actually have parts in a far more readily discernible way than the sun; and the sun is far more obviously different from everything else than a wagon from a cart or a tumbril or a chariot. Whether Plato drew the correct conclusion from his arguments is another matter. He might have concluded that there is in fact no difference between true opinion of an object (in the sense that excludes opinion *about* it) and knowledge of an object (in the sense that excludes knowledge *that*), since the criterion common to both is simply the ability to recognize. But examination of the *Theaetetus* has shown that in it there is no evidence that Plato was aware of the distinctions which could lead him to

4-2

formulate such a conclusion. In the *Theaetetus*, Plato believes both that knowledge is of simples and that such knowledge is different from true opinion.

The *Theaetetus*, however, does not answer the further and more interesting question of exactly what Plato did think knowledge to be. Some hint is perhaps afforded by the digression on philosophy and rhetoric; but the digression, as we saw, gives only a hint and not an exposition. There is nothing in the *Theaetetus* which entails the conclusion that Plato had discarded the epistemology of the *Republic*, but equally there is nothing which makes it certain that he could not have modified it. The general impression left by the *Theaetetus* is that Plato continued to think of knowledge as a sort of mental seeing or touching.[1] In English, of course, we can speak quite naturally of 'grasping a problem' or 'seeing a point of view'. But the metaphor is one which stands for understanding a proposition, not knowing an object. Plato, however, seems to think of a state of knowledge as one in which the mind (or soul) is experiencing an absolutely clear apprehension of certain particular things, such as the concepts of existence, beauty and so on which are cited by Plato to refute the equation of perception and knowledge and which the mind is described as seeing (186A σκοπεῖσθαι) by means of its reasoning (ἀναλογιζομένη). This notion also makes it easier to understand Plato's worries about error. For although it is quite conceivable that someone should, for instance, mistake Theaetetus for Socrates when the light is not too good and he is rather a long way away in any case, how are we to explain a mistake in arithmetic in which there is no reason to suppose that the mind cannot perfectly well see the objects which it then proceeds to confuse with each other? It was not until the *Sophist* that Plato saw that the question could only be answered by being approached in a different way and that the problem of non-existence could for this purpose, at least, be by-passed with the help of the Form of Otherness.

Whether, however, the *Sophist* led Plato to modify his conception of knowledge as ultimately intuitive, and to emancipate himself from the assimilation of all types of knowledge to knowledge by acquaintance, is a question to which it is difficult to give an unequivocal answer. There is no discussion of knowledge as such in the *Sophist*, although there is a brief description of the science of dialectic and a reference to

[1] See p. 10, n. 2.

the philosopher's region (τόπος), which is presumably the ὑπερουράνιος τόπος of the *Phaedrus*. Plato only remarks that 'in some such region we shall now and later find the philosopher, if we look for him' (253 E). The subsequent discussion in the *Sophist* will be considered in due course; but if Plato intended to write a dialogue entitled the *Philosopher* which was to follow the *Politicus*, this 'now and later' could be plausibly regarded as looking forward to it. The evidence for this is strong, but not certain.[1] In addition to this passage of the *Sophist*, there are three passages in the *Politicus* which are taken to predict the *Philosopher*. In effect, they are all part of the preliminary passage in which the programme for the dialogue is agreed. The dialogue opens at 257 A with the remark of Socrates to Theodorus that he is very grateful for his introduction to Theaetetus and the Eleatic stranger. Theodorus replies by telling Socrates that he will be three times as grateful when they have defined the statesman and philosopher for him as well as the sophist. Then at 257 B Theodorus asks the stranger if he would now prefer to define the statesman or the philosopher. Finally, at 258 A, Socrates says that young Socrates will reply to him on another occasion. Cornford, followed by Skemp, argues that in the unwritten *Philosopher* Socrates was to be the questioner and young Socrates the respondent. This deduction, however, must remain very uncertain, for although such an arrangement is envisaged at *Pol.* 258 A the two previous remarks in this passage and the remark of the stranger at *Soph.* 253 E surely imply that it is the stranger himself who will produce the definition of the philosopher as well as those of the sophist and statesman. But it remains at least possible that whoever would have been the *dramatis personae* Plato did intend to write the *Philosopher*. It is unlikely that these hints are purely irrelevant or accidental; and the *Philosopher*, if written, would presumably have contained some explicit exposition of the philosopher's knowledge and the means by which it is acquired. That the dialogue should not be written after Plato's third visit to Sicily is plausible enough, particularly in view of the distrust in the written word reflected in the *Seventh Letter* (if genuine). No very confident conclusions can be drawn from

---

[1] See Cornford, pp. 168–70, Skemp, pp. 20–2; also A. Diès, *Parménide³* (Paris, 1956), pp. xiv–xvii. Young Socrates, the respondent of the *Politicus* and proposed respondent of the *Philosopher*, is mentioned by Plato at *Theaet.* 147D, *Soph.* 218B, and (if genuine) *Ep. XI* 358D; also by Aristotle at *Met.* 1036b25.

all this. But if Plato did in fact have the *Philosopher* in mind, then it is not surprising that the later dialogues contain no explicit expression of Plato's theory of knowledge or that there is no direct reference to the Theory of Forms as such.

Plato's only explicit discussion of knowledge after the writing of the *Theaetetus* apart from *Philebus* 61 D 10–E 4 is in the *Seventh Letter* (342 A ff.); but since its authenticity is not beyond question[1] no strong reliance can be placed upon conclusions deduced from it. If, however, it is genuine, it offers conclusive evidence that Plato in the last decade of his life believed that ultimate knowledge is the intuitive apprehension of the truly real. It confirms the conclusion of the *Cratylus* that names are inadequate to yield knowledge of their nominees; and further, it declares that knowledge about things such as is embodied in definitions compounded out of words must always be inferior to knowledge of things in themselves. Phenomenal knowledge (περὶ ταῦτα or τὸ ποῖόν τι) is bracketed with true opinion in a category still inferior to true knowledge of τὸ ὄν. This final knowledge may result from exercise in the manipulation and comparison of the four preceding categories (name, definition, sensible instance and phenomenal knowledge), but it is itself a full intuitive cognition of (in the example actually given) the Form of Circle itself.

Unless, however, the *Seventh Letter* comes to be firmly and finally established as genuine—and it is difficult to see how any really conclusive demonstration of its authenticity can be possible—it cannot be cited as proof of Plato's later views. It is perhaps still evidence of a kind. But its forger, if there was one, could either have been ignorant of Plato's later views or have deliberately chosen to disregard them. It is only safe to say that its genuineness seems sufficiently possible for it to lend a further probability to the view that Plato's highest knowledge remained an intuition of supremely existent objects. The distinction between this and phenomenal knowledge is explicitly asserted, as we have seen, at the end of the *Philebus*. For evidence from Plato's own writings as to his final views, it is necessary to consider such meagre hints as are afforded in the *Laws*.

There are only three passages in the *Laws* which give some slight

---

[1] The most persuasive advocate for its genuineness is Bluck (*Plato. The Seventh and Eighth Letters*, Cambridge, 1947), but his arguments have not found universal acceptance.

indication of Plato's latest views on the nature of knowledge.[1] From none can any certain conclusion be drawn, but they seem to point away from the likelihood of any modification of an earlier view that true knowledge is apprehension of an object. In the first (875 C–D), knowledge is described as above law and custom. In the second (895 D), the distinction is drawn between knowledge of the essence (οὐσία) of something, knowledge of the definition of the essence (λόγος) and knowledge of the name (ὄνομα). In the third (965 B–966 A), which occurs in the last few pages of Book XII, the most exact examination and contemplation of anything is said to be to look at the one idea gathered from many particular things. These passages cannot be regarded as conclusive. But they are strongly reminiscent of views expressed by Plato elsewhere; and if Plato had in fact discarded his earlier belief in knowledge by acquaintance of Forms, it would be extremely surprising to find them, stated as they are. Indeed, precisely because they are so cursory, it is likely that they have reference to views which Plato's readers would know him to continue to hold. If he had radically modified his views on the nature of knowledge, it would be natural to expect either no such apparent references to his earlier views or else some longer exposition from which it would be clear that the intuitive apprehension of Forms was no longer being referred to. The conclusion, then, is that the *Laws* offers no evidence of an abandonment by Plato of his belief that the highest knowledge is intuition of Forms, and in fact some indication to the contrary.

Finally, there remains whatever evidence might be drawn from what we know of Plato's unwritten doctrines. This fearful question is fortunately outside the scope of the present essay. But without enter-

---

[1] Though only three times in any sense discussed, knowledge is, of course, fairly frequently mentioned in the *Laws*. Several times this is knowledge how, e.g. at 679C, 689D, 813 E; but nothing can be argued from these passages. The important distinction between theoretical and practical knowledge first made by Plato at *Pol.* 258 C–D is never followed up, or at least not to any explicit distinction between knowing how and knowing that. Indeed, statesmanship is quickly assimilated to theoretical knowledge and there is no subsequent consideration of the difference between intellectual knowledge and practical skill. In one somewhat surprising passage of the *Laws*, ἐπιστῆμαι are bracketed with δόξαι as well as logos as the natural rulers of the soul (689 B). But this need not in any way suggest that knowledge and opinion are still not radically different to Plato. The point being made is the rationality of the soul; and by this criterion, knowledge and opinion are on the same side (as against the passions). The distinction between theoretical and practical knowledge is found by Taylor (*Plato*⁶, London, 1949, p. 53) at *Charm.* 165 E–166 A. But I agree with Gould (p. 38) and Vlastos (p. 229, n. 7) that this is an unwarrantable interpretation.

ing into it, it is still possible briefly to summarize its bearing on the problem under discussion. It seems clear that the content of the Lecture (or lectures) on the Good was largely mathematical.[1] Further, if Plato gave any oral teaching in addition to the Lecture on the Good, it seems that this too was largely devoted to mathematics and to the correlation or assimilation of Forms and Ideal Numbers.[2] This last question must remain uncertain despite the frequent assertions of Aristotle that the Forms were numbers,[3] but the implications for Plato's later views on the nature of knowledge may be safely put forward. If it is true that Plato in later life expounded an unwritten doctrine, and if this doctrine was even somewhat as described by Aristotle, then Plato's metaphysics came increasingly to be based on an intuitive knowledge of the nature of the Ideal Numbers. If, therefore, any conclusion at all can be drawn from the evidence for Plato's unwritten doctrines, it is that the highest knowledge remained for him knowledge of those objects which he thought to possess the most exalted ontological status.

There is thus no really positive evidence for Plato's latest epistemological views (unless, of course, the *Timaeus* is taken as indisputably written only very shortly before the *Laws*, in which case it could be regarded as certain that the *Theaetetus* and *Sophist* brought about no serious modification of Plato's earlier beliefs). However, even without reliance on a late dating for the *Timaeus*, such evidence as can be gathered tends to support the unequivocal statement of the *Philebus* (61D–E) that the truest knowledge is knowledge of τὰ κατὰ ταὐτὰ καὶ ὡσαύτως ὄντα ἀεί. Knowledge, on the other hand, is not only of Forms; and that Plato did not think that it was when he wrote the *Theaetetus* has been shown from study of the *Theaetetus* itself. The contrast between phenomenal and absolute knowledge is nowhere stated in the *Theaetetus* as it is in the *Philebus*. However, it may perhaps be deduced from contrasting the final argument (logos as the

---

[1] Aristoxenus, *Harm.* II, 30–1; Simplicius, *in Phys.* 453.25–455.14. See further Ross, pp. 142–53 arguing against Cherniss (3).

[2] A clear and useful discussion of these problems is given by Ross (pp. 176–220). If there existed also in the Academy a written collection of Divisions (*Ep. XIII* 360B, Arist. *De Part. An.* 642b10–13, *De Gen. et Corr.* 330b13–17) these presumably were not concerned with mathematics, although certain scholars have attempted to relate the method of division to Plato's generation of the numbers (Ross, pp. 194–205).

[3] For references see Ross, p. 216, n. 1, although some of these passages need not refer to Plato himself.

ability to give the essential differentness) with the digression on philosophy and rhetoric. For in the final argument, although it is tacitly assumed that knowledge of Theaetetus is possible, Theaetetus is clearly not a Form. He is presumably a partial instantiation of several Forms such as Beauty and Manhood (this point will become important in the *Sophist*), but this is hardly the same thing. On the other hand the philosopher is described in the digression as spending his labours on the question not of his next-door neighbour but of what Man[1] is and what distinguishes his nature from that of others (174 B). It is possible that Plato came to assimilate phenomenal knowledge and true opinion (cf. *Ep. VII* 342 C 4–5); and indeed, as we have already seen, it is a good deal harder to see what the difference might be between true opinion and phenomenal knowledge of an object than between true opinion and phenomenal knowledge of a fact. Plato never makes himself clear on this point, and perhaps he was in fact confused about it in his own mind. But in the *Theaetetus* he makes it clear that there is a difference between true opinion and knowledge of an object; and there is nothing to suggest that he did not believe that the highest knowledge, with which the philosopher is concerned, is knowledge of Forms.

This does not mean, however, that we are required to believe with Cornford that the dialogue is intended to recommend the Forms by withholding them. Grounds have already been given for rejecting Cornford's view; and, in fact, nothing has emerged from the examination of the dialogue which requires the abandonment of the view originally suggested by a preliminary consideration of its lay-out and content. Plato sets out to achieve three objects. First, he shows that knowledge can be equated neither with perception, nor true opinion, nor true opinion plus logos. Second, he considers the problem of error, as he had done in the *Euthydemus* and *Cratylus*, but is still unable to solve it. Third, he gives a reminder but not an exposition of the region in which the true philosopher operates. There is no reason to conclude from this that Plato no longer believed that true knowledge is of Forms. On the other hand, there is no need to draw from this conclusion the further conclusion that in the discussion of error he was merely setting problems to which he had the Theory of Forms as a solution up his sleeve. There is no mention in the *Theaetetus* of the

[1] For the Form of Man, cf. *Parm.* 130 C, *Phil.* 15 A.

method of diaeresis; and it is this method, exemplified in the examination of the relations between the μέγιστα γένη as well as the technique of dichotomous division, which gave Plato the solution to the problem of error expounded in the *Theaetetus* and the problem of the intercommunion of Forms expounded in the *Parmenides*. If the *Phaedrus* was written between the *Theaetetus* and *Sophist*, Plato had presumably not yet fully developed it. If the *Phaedrus* was written before the *Theaetetus*, he may not yet have seen how consideration of the relation between the highest Forms could yield an answer to the problem of thinking what is not. It is this problem, unsolved in the *Theaetetus*, to which the *Sophist* sets out to find the answer; and it is to the *Sophist* that we must now turn.

III

THE 'SOPHIST': ONTOLOGY AND LOGIC

At the opening of the *Sophist*, Theaetetus, Theodorus and Socrates are represented as meeting again on the morning following the discussion reported in the *Theaetetus*. Theodorus opens the conversation by introducing a Stranger from Elea whom he describes as a member of the school of Parmenides and Zeno and 'very much a philosopher' (216A μάλα δὲ ἄνδρα φιλόσοφον). It is this Stranger who becomes the protagonist in the subsequent discussion. Commentators have speculated on Plato's choice of an Eleatic as the mouthpiece of important arguments of his own. However, all that matters for the purpose of interpreting the dialogue is to be certain that these arguments are seriously meant by Plato. Apart from the interest and significance of the arguments themselves, this is made clear by the introductory remarks put into the mouth of Theodorus. Socrates expresses the fear that the Stranger may turn out to be a merely eristic disputant, 'a god of refutation' (216B). But Theodorus reasserts that he is a genuine philosopher, and Socrates (who pays an incidental tribute to Parmenides himself) persuades the Stranger to embark on a definition of either the Sophist, the Statesman or the Philosopher. The Stranger selects the Sophist as his topic and Theaetetus as his respondent. The search for the definition of the Sophist then proceeds (218D).

Thus the whole dialogue is directed ostensibly to the attempt to define the Sophist; and the method used for this purpose is the method of diaeresis. An illustrative definition of the Angler is first given from 218E to 221C. Preliminary attempts to define the Sophist are then undertaken until 231B. Here the results so far arrived at are reviewed. The Stranger expresses particular interest in the description of the Sophist as a controversialist (232B ἀντιλογικός). This leads to a discussion of how the Sophist can deceive his pupils by means of what is only an apparent knowledge. He is duly classified as an imitator or maker of images, but the art of image-making (235B εἰδωλοποιική) is then divided into the making of likenesses (εἰκαστική) and the making of semblances, or apparent likenesses (φανταστική). The Stranger expresses uncertainty as to which of these the Sophist is to be placed under (236C–D). He then points out that the extremely difficult question has now been raised of seeming without being and saying what is not true (236D–E); and he quotes the dictum of Parmenides that it will never be proved that things that are not are. It is the resolution of this problem which occupies almost all the remainder of the dialogue (237B–264B). Only then is the definition by division of the Sophist resumed, and the final definition given (264C–268D).

The definition by division is interesting for the light it throws on Plato's method of division as such. But this is a topic outside the scope of the present study; and the most philosophically important part of the *Sophist* is the section in which the dictum of Parmenides is circumvented. One preliminary point, however, should be made which arises out of the importance attached by Plato to his divisions. Not only is the method taken very seriously by Plato himself, but it assumes the pre-existence of an ontological structure which the true philosopher can ascertain. Although it may be regarded as in some sense a procedure of naming (cf., for instance, *Soph.* 267D), this procedure is in no way an arbitrary one. There is one passage in the *Sophist* which might suggest that it is: at 222B, where the definition is being put forward of the Sophist as a hunter of the tame animal Man, the Stranger tells Theaetetus to proceed as he pleases (θὲς δὲ ὅπῃ χαίρεις). But it is clear that the point is simply that the Stranger wishes to extract from Theaetetus some tentative suggestion which may then be followed up or rejected. Nothing is said to the effect that one suggestion will be as legitimate or valid as another. The method of division does not mark any concession by Plato to νόμος at the expense of φύσις any more than did the rejection of a nature-theory of names in the *Cratylus*. Names can be true or false, as is reasserted at *Pol.* 281A; and in the *Politicus* Plato is at pains to point out that divisions can be incorrectly made.[1] Moreover, to make such incorrect divisions is not

---

[1] *Pol.* 262C ff. There is dispute as to exactly why Plato considered such divisions as Greeks/non-Greeks invalid, but it seems clear that he is denying the status of Forms to such notions as not-Greek and not-ten-thousand. Alexander, *in Met.* 80.18–81.13, gives as examples of Forms not recognized by the Academy not-man, not-musical, not-horse, not-wood and not-white. The difficulties raised by *Soph.* 257D–258C will be discussed later. It is sometimes suggested that Plato rejects not-Greek as a Form on extensional

merely to offer unilluminating suggestions for the subdivision of genera into species, but to misrepresent the true structure of reality. For Plato such a question as 'is a crocodile a fish?' can be settled not by reference to a lexicographer or an ichthyologist, but only a philosopher.

There are, of course, a great many more problems than this arising out of the method of diaeresis. In fact, it is questionable whether we ought not to distinguish between two or even three different methods of diaeresis as employed by Plato. The examination of the interrelations between the μέγιστα γένη of the *Sophist* cannot, as Stenzel believed it could, be regarded as an exercise on a higher level of the same kind as the search for the Sophist and Statesman. Stenzel pictures a sort of ontological pyramid in which all other Forms are subordinated to the Form of Being. But in the first place, the relations between the μέγιστα γένη are not those of genus and species; and in the second, there is nothing in the relevant passages of the *Sophist* to suggest that any of the μέγιστα γένη is logically or otherwise superior to any or all of the others. Apart from this, there is the further difference between, say, the relation of Man to Animal[1] and the relation of Red to Colour.[2] For whereas Redness is a colour, Manhood is not an animal; and whereas men differ from horses by virtue of rationality,[3] for instance, or the fact of having only two feet, the difference between red and green or green and blue is clearly one of a different kind, much less

grounds; that is to say, that because there are more barbarians than Greeks, such a division is not properly δίχα just as a division of numbers into ten thousand and not-ten-thousand is not properly δίχα. This would presumably mean that if the non-Greek world were sufficiently depopulated by the plague, then a Form of Barbarian would come into existence. It is possible that Plato simply had not thought of this. But it is more likely that he rejected not-Greek and not-ten-thousand as Forms simply because (following the analysis of negation in the *Sophist*) such terms mean no more than 'different from Greek' and 'different from ten thousand'; and it is Difference which is a Form.

[1] This relation is discussed in the *Timaeus* (30C, 39E). It raises the difficult question of how far Plato failed to distinguish between Forms and their extensions, which is not relevant here. But there is evidence in the *Politicus* that Plato did not effectively make the distinction, although the orthodox view of the method of divisions understands it as concerned only with genus, species and sub-species. On this point I am indebted to Mr J. M. E. Moravcsik for permission to consult an unpublished paper.

[2] The subdivision of Colour is cited by Plato in the *Philebus* at 12E in order to argue for a similar subdivision of Pleasure. The subdivisions (μέρη) of Shape are also cited (12E–13A). It is sometimes argued that the *Philebus* marks the inception by Plato of a whole new methodology; but it is perhaps more appropriate to see it as a further development of the method of diaeresis.

[3] Thus the possession of knowledge is what distinguishes the Philosopher from the Sophist (*Soph.* 235A, 253C–254B, 268B–C).

susceptible to the imposition of a dichotomous conceptual framework such as is employed in the search for the Sophist or the Statesman. It is extremely difficult to determine how far Plato was aware of these differences. But for the purpose of the present essay what is important to note is that however great these differences and however much Plato was aware of them, the method always assumes a pre-existing structure which dialectic enables the philosopher to ascertain. Nor is this assumption modified by the passage of the *Politicus* (285 D) in which Plato declares that the method is important less because it throws light on the problem under discussion than because it makes those who practise it better dialecticians. The method still enables the philosopher to determine the true nature of the Statesman; and although 'no sensible man would wish to pursue the definition of weaving for its own sake', the attempt must lose whatever point it has if there is no right definition to which the method can lead, whether of weaving or anything else.

The significance of all this for the *Sophist* is that all its questions are, for Plato, ultimately ontological questions. Plato is not concerned to propose a set of logical axioms or to select a conceptual framework but to determine the nature, properties and capacity for interrelation of certain selected Forms.[1] His own description of the science of dialectic is given in the *Sophist* at 253D–E. Here the method by which the Sophist is being defined is explictly bracketed with the method which determines the interrelations between the μέγιστα γένη. The method as a whole is summarized in the single compact sentence which runs from 253D5 to 253E2. This sentence Cornford[2] seems to understand as referring to Forms alone; but it is clear that in the first of the four procedures described (μίαν ἰδέαν διὰ πολλῶν, ἑνὸς ἑκάστου κειμένου χωρίς, πάντη διατεταμένην ἱκανῶς διαισθάνεται), πολλῶν refers to particulars, for if it did not then ἑνὸς ἑκάστου should read μιᾶς ἑκάστης. Plato appears in this brief exposition to be giving a total summary of

---

[1] Hamlyn makes the interesting suggestion (Hamlyn (1), p. 292) that a parallel might be drawn between Plato's doctrine of communion of Forms and Carnap's concept of *L*-range (R. Carnap, *Introduction to Semantics* (Harvard, 1942), pp. 95 ff.). But Carnap's concept of *L*-range is based upon distinctions such as those between atomic and molecular propositions and between extensional and non-extensional language which would be totally beyond Plato's conception. Such a parallel is therefore more likely to mislead than to illuminate, although it does serve to show that the problems confronting Plato and contemporary philosophers are in some sense still the same.

[2] Cornford, pp. 267–8.

his new philosophical method. Moreover, the language in which he introduces and comments on it should of itself serve as an effective rebuttal to any argument that he did not himself attach very great importance to the method. This may be further supported by the remarks of Socrates in the *Phaedrus* (266c) where the new method has been first introduced, and by the terms in which it is again (though somewhat differently) described in the *Philebus* (16c–17a).[1] Dialectic, after the *Phaedrus*, involves the ascertaining of the nature of the Forms not by the method of hypothesis but by ascertaining their relations to each other. It is in this that the whole of the *Sophist* is an exercise.

We may now return to the point in the argument at which the attempted definition of the *Sophist* was shown to involve the problem of what is not. The Eleatic Stranger, after quoting the dictum of Parmenides, suggests that the discussion should now proceed by considering this dictum on its own merits (237b). He remarks that we do not hesitate to utter the phrase 'that which is not at all' (τὸ μηδαμῶς ὄν). He then opens the examination of Parmenides' dictum by considering precisely this phrase.

Before, however, proceeding to look more closely at the Stranger's argument, it is necessary to issue a preliminary caveat of some importance. It is commonly assumed[2] that Plato in the *Sophist* distinguishes between the existential sense of εἶναι and at least one other sense. But this assumption is dangerously misleading. What can be far more readily assumed is that Plato marks off the identitative sense from at least one other, for Identity (τὸ ταὐτόν) is explicitly distinguished from Being (τὸ ὄν) as a separate Form. But this fact by itself already suggests what closer study of Plato's discussion of Being will confirm, namely that Plato's analysis depends upon the assimilation of the existential and copulative senses of εἶναι. This is not to say that Plato, whether consciously or unconsciously, altogether obliterates the difference. There are grounds for arguing that this is at any rate not entirely the case. But any translation of εἶναι as 'exist' or τὸ ὄν as 'existence' at once begs a question whose answer is likely to be the

---

[1] Further support may perhaps be enlisted from the notorious Epicrates fragment (Kock, vol. II, p. 287) which describes the exercise conducted in the Academy. Not very much reliance can be placed upon it; but it is hard to believe that we should so thoroughly discount it as Professor Cherniss would have us do (Cherniss (3), p. 63).

[2] Cornford, p. 296; Ackrill (2), p. 1.

opposite. Accordingly, it is necessary in all contexts to begin by translating εἶναι simply as 'be' even when (as at 250A11 or 254D10) 'exist' would at first be the natural rendering.

THE DISCUSSION OF NON-BEING

The Stranger's opening argument runs from 237B to 239B. Its result is to expose the difficulty involved in speaking of 'that which is not' at all. The argument falls into two parts. In the first (237B–E) it is shown that the phrase cannot properly be applied to anything, since anything which can be designated as 'something' must require that being should be ascribed to it. In the second part (238A–239B) it is shown that no name or attribute[1] can be ascribed to 'what is not' since such ascription will involve the ascription of being to what by definition cannot have any. The conclusion is that what has no being at all not only cannot be thought or spoken of (238C) but cannot even be spoken of as being incapable of being spoken of (239A). Here, then, are the roots of the doctrine nicknamed by Quine[2] 'Plato's beard', which has continued to exercise a persistent propensity to dull the edge of Occam's razor. We wish to speak of what is not. But for us to be able to do so there must be something of which we can say that it is not. But how can there be, since all that we wish to say about it is that it is not something, or indeed anything at all? And so on.

At this point, it does not greatly matter whether Plato distinguished the existential sense of εἶναι from any other. Even if he thought that to be means in all cases to be something or other, it is still the problem of non-existence which he is here discussing. For he is discussing what is not anything at all; and indeed it is precisely this which lands him in such difficulties. The non-existent (i.e. what is not anything at all) cannot even be unthinkable or unsayable, for to be unthinkable or unsayable it must be something (i.e. it must exist). Thus Plato seems to find himself forced to the conclusion that τὸ μηδαμῶς ὄν is a meaningless phrase, and therefore that everything referable must in some sense exist. τὸ μηδαμῶς ὄν itself must be regarded as a sort of pretend-

---

[1] Whether or not Plato distinguished these two does not affect the argument. The examples given (which recall Socrates' 'dream' in the *Theaetetus*) are 'one', 'the', 'it', and 'being'. Cornford (p. 207, n. 2) proposes to read τὸ 'τό' at 239A3, but this is not necessary. See also p. 41, n. 1 above.

[2] W. V. Quine, *From a Logical Point of View* (Harvard, 1953), ch. 1, 'On What There Is'.

reference, a phrase which purports to name something but does not in fact name anything at all. Accordingly, Parmenides' dictum is circumvented by translating 'what is not' into 'what is not X' in all cases. The results of the examination of Parmenides' dictum are later summarized at 258 E–259 A. The Stranger there remarks that 'we have long ago said good-bye to the question of the opposite of Being'. The other non-being, whose being has been satisfactorily vindicated, is the Form of Difference which participates in Being, but yet is not (i.e. is not identical with) the Being in which it participates.

But of course the fact remains that although others besides Plato have sought to maintain the view that everything exists, it is a view which there are strong intuitive grounds for rejecting. If it is the case that $(x) (Ex)$—an assertion a good deal more drastic, it should be noted, than Quine's notorious contention that to be is to be the value of a variable, which as stated need mean no more than $Ex \rightarrow (\exists y) (y = x)$, or that 'something is x'—then we at once forfeit the right to say that either mermaids do not exist or that Odysseus, if he existed, would have been an interesting person to talk to. Precisely because we in fact do wish to make statements of this kind, we wish to maintain that $\sim (x) (\Diamond Ex \supset Ex)$, a view directly contrary to the position Plato seems to be adopting in the *Sophist*. In answer to our claim to place mermaids among the class of non-existents, Plato might wish to assert, as some philosophers have wished to do, that what we are trying to say is that mermaids are not spatio-temporal entities but merely ideas or images. Indeed, there is even some evidence that this is precisely what Plato would say, for in the *Republic* he describes chimaeras as composite images made up of images of spatio-temporally existing creatures (588 C–D).[1] But this will not do. For the entities whose existence we wish to deny are not ideas of mermaids and chimaeras but spatio-temporal mermaids and chimaeras. I do not myself believe that mermaids exist; but I am prepared to believe that they might; and if someone were to tell me that he had found a mermaid in his swimming-pool I should certainly not understand him to mean that he had found an image or idea of a mermaid in his swimming-pool. If this is in fact the move which Plato would wish to make when faced with the problem of mermaids, there is evidence that Aristotle at least was not convinced by it, since he is represented by Alexander (*in Met.* 82.1–

[1] Cf. Diog. Laert. VII, 53.

7) as rejecting the λόγος ὁ ἀπὸ τοῦ νοεῖν as a proof of the Forms by citing the fact that centaurs, although we think of them, are non-existent. But Plato's answer would perhaps be simply to assign mermaids and the rest to an appropriate place in his own gradational ontology. Everything has some sort of being; but mermaids, since they have for the moment no instantiations in the world, have even less being than sensible particulars.

All this, however, is largely speculative. In the discussion of τὸ μηδαμῶς ὄν in the *Sophist* Plato, although he goes on in an interesting and important passage to discuss the ontological status of images, does not explicitly consider mermaids or chimaeras or centaurs or anything of the kind. Still less does he consider round squares or the present king of France. His concern is not with what there is or might be, but only with what is not. In this first argument arising from Parmenides' dictum he begins by considering what is not in the sense of what does not have any being whatsoever and concludes that it cannot be dealt with at all. He is well aware, as the Stranger's original question makes clear (237B), that τὸ μηδαμῶς ὄν is a phrase which we have no initial hesitation in uttering. But the subsequent argument shows that to think of it as denoting what cannot, if the phrase is to serve its intended purpose, be there to be denoted or even to be declared to be un-denotable makes it impossible to discuss the question of it in any way at all. However, we must beware of any unqualified assertion that Plato concluded from this that everything mentionable exists. For we are again faced with the difficulty, already discussed in the consideration of the *Theaetetus*, that for Plato some things could exist more than others. Whatever view we may wish to hold on the logic of designation and existence,[1] existence is never a matter of degree. But in Plato's case it is only safe to say that in the *Sophist* he appears to take up the position that everything mentionable has some sort of being. Whether, on the other hand, he emancipates himself from the equation of existence and reality and the unequivocally gradational ontology of the *Republic* is a question which depends on the argument in the *Sophist* which follows the discussion of τὸ μηδαμῶς ὄν.

[1] For recent discussion of the subject see Quine, *op. cit.*, esp. chs. I, VI, and IX; also e.g. H. S. Leonard, 'The Logic of Existence', *Philosophical Studies* VII (1956), pp. 49–64, and N. Rescher, 'On the Logic of Existence and Denotation', *Philosophical Review* LXVIII (1959), pp. 157–80, to which I am indebted for the formulation of some of my general remarks.

THE DISCUSSION OF IMAGES

The Stranger concludes his discussion of τὸ μηδαμῶς ὄν by suggesting (239 B) to Theaetetus that it is now his turn to attempt to say something legitimate about it without attributing being or unity or plurality to it. Theaetetus, however, observes sensibly enough (239 C) that such an undertaking would require a remarkable zeal in view of the result of the Stranger's own attempt. The Stranger accordingly turns to the question of images (εἴδωλα), since it is the art of creating these which has been attributed to the Sophist. Theaetetus suggests that images are reflections in water or mirrors, or images such as paintings or sculptures (239 D). In fact, he makes the same mistake which he made at the beginning of the *Theaetetus* when he was asked to give a definition of knowledge and instead produced a series of examples of knowledge. The Stranger accordingly asks him to give the common characteristic of the instances which he was prepared to list under the single heading of 'image' (240 A). Theaetetus then gives the definition of an image as 'something else of the same sort which is a likeness of the real thing'. This definition is then discussed in a brief but important passage (240 A9–240 C6) of which it will be as well to offer a full translation. Unfortunately there is an uncertainty in the text at two points, which will require discussion. However, the translation of Burnet's text runs as follows:

240 A9 STR. When you say 'something else of the same sort' do you mean
240 B1 another real thing (ἀληθινόν)? Or what do you understand the phrase to refer to?
TH. I certainly do not mean a real thing, but something like it.
STR. Do you mean by 'real' truly existent (ὄντως ὄν)?
TH. Yes.
5 STR. Well, then. By 'not real' do you mean the opposite of truly real (ἀληθές)?
TH. Of course.
STR. So by 'what is like' (τὸ ἐοικός) you mean what is not truly existent, if you are going to speak of it as not real.
TH. But it has at any rate existence of a kind (ἔστι γε μὴν πως).
10 STR. But not real existence, according to you.
TH. No indeed, except in that it is really (ὄντως) a likeness.
STR. Then although it is not really existent (ὄντως ὄν) it really is what we call a likeness?

5-2

C1   TH. Some such combination of not real and real (τὸ μὴ ὂν τῷ ὄντι) does seem to have been put together; and very strange it is.

The difficulty in the text is the possible occurrence of an additional οὐκ at 240 B 7 (οὐκ ὄντως οὐκ ὂν ἄρα λέγεις τὸ ἐοικός) and again at B 12 (οὐκ ὂν ἄρα οὐκ ὄντως ἐστὶν ὄντως ἦν λέγομεν εἰκόνα). Both are rejected by Burnet, who is followed by Cornford. Campbell retains the second but not the first. Diès and Friedländer retain both. There can be little question that the rejection of both gives the easiest and most immediately satisfactory sense. But the *lectio difficilior* is well attested;[1] and it is not too readily explicable how it should have become established in place of οὐκ ὄντως ὂν by the fifth century A.D.[2] Nor need 240 B 7-8 be read as a question if the second οὐκ is retained, which is what Cornford maintains.[3] If the second οὐκ is retained, οὐκ ὄντως οὐκ ὂν must be taken to mean 'not really non-existent'. The phrase is a curious one, since we should presumably expect οὐκ ὄντως μὴ ὄν, if anything. But if we should in fact retain the reading transmitted by the best medieval codices, this is the sense which the phrase must bear. The argument must then be that a likeness is neither a real thing (240 B 2) nor a really unreal thing; that is to say, not to be assigned to the class of τὸ μηδαμῶς ὄν discussed in the preceding argument. 240 B 12 can then be taken as 'not really being non-existent, it really is what we call a likeness'. It cannot be denied that the retention of the second οὐκ makes both sentences read somewhat awkwardly. But it does not make either of them read nonsensically; and it must remain at least an open question whether the retention ought not to be made.

Fortunately, however, the interpretation of the argument as a whole does not depend on the definite acceptance of one or other of the readings. It is clear that its purpose is to show that a likeness is in some sense both real (ὄν) and unreal (μὴ ὄν). What it is important to determine is in precisely what sense Plato believed this to be so. We have already had occasion to notice that Plato does not draw any clear distinctions between existent, real and true. It is of course the case that a statue, for instance, is in fact as truly existent as a man and, although not a real man, is a perfectly real statue. Moreover, it is not

---

[1] For a fuller discussion and a defence of οὐκ ὄντως οὐκ ὂν see Kohnke, esp. pp. 35, 37-8.

[2] Kohnke (p. 35) cites Proclus, *In Parm.* 744, 31; 816, 18; 842, 7 (Cousin).

[3] Cornford, p. 211, n. 1.

inconceivable that Plato should come to express a recognition of this. He has a word which he could use for real (as opposed to imaginary), namely ἀληθινός; he has a word which he could use for existent (as opposed to non-existent), namely ὄν; and he has a word which he could use for true (as opposed to false), namely ἀληθής. Thus if he became disposed to abandon his assimilation of existence and reality and his conception of them as something to be understood as a question of degree, he did in fact possess a language capable of expressing the necessary distinctions. He could have said that an εἰκὼν οὐκ ἀληθινῶς ἐστὶν ἐκεῖνο οὗ ἐστιν εἰκών, ἀλλ' ἀληθινῶς ἐστὶν εἰκών· καὶ ὡς ἀληθινὴ οὖσα εἰκών, ὄντως ἐστὶν ὄν. But examination of the argument as it is in fact presented shows that Plato says nothing of the kind. For although he says that a likeness not only is not but also is (in that it really is an image), he does not say that to be an image is to be (or exist) just as truly (or really) as to be an original. In developing the argument, the Stranger does not attempt to induce Theaetetus to recant his assertion that a likeness is not ἀληθινόν: not only is this initial statement un-questioned throughout the argument, but the equation of ἀληθινόν and ὄντως ὄν is similarly unquestioned. The argument only sets out to establish that a likeness has some sort of existence by virtue of being a likeness. To this final point it may perhaps be objected that the πως of 240 B 9 need not be required to bear this sense: it is possible that it need mean only that a likeness somehow must exist rather than that a like-ness must exist to some (limited) extent. However, that this second sense should in fact be understood seems to be made clear from the following line, which shows that εἶναί πως is to be contrasted with ἀληθινῶς εἶναι.[1] This view may be finally confirmed by 240 B 12 where (if we follow Burnet's text) a likeness is said to be really (ὄντως) a likeness but still not to be really (ὄντως) ὄν. The conclusion, therefore, is that this argument cannot be interpreted to mark any recantation by Plato of his gradational ontology. Its purpose is only to show that a likeness must have some sort of existence in so far as it is capable of being a likeness at all; and this conclusion follows naturally enough from the previous argument which showed that nothing can be aseptically assigned to the class of absolutely non-existents, not even τὸ μηδαμῶς ὄν itself. On the other hand, a likeness is also μὴ ὄν in so

[1] Cf. Tim. 52 c οὐσίας ἁμωσγέπως ἀντεχομένην as opposed to ὄντως ὄν. For the assimila-tion of falsehood to imitation (and not in respect of statements) cf. Phil. 40 c.

far as it is not ἀληθινόν. The result is thus that, as Theaetetus observes, ὄν and μὴ ὄν are strangely compounded together.

The Stranger now concludes (240C) that the Sophist 'has forced us unwillingly to admit that τὸ μὴ ὄν has some sort of being'. This, however, is still a long way from circumventing the dictum of Parmenides. All that has been established is that the semblance (φάντασμα) by which the Sophist is enabled to practise his art of deception appears to have some sort of being as well as some sort of non-being. It is the effect of this art that our minds come to think what is false. The problem of falsehood is then fully stated (240D–241B). It should perhaps be pointed out that the Sophist's semblance is not, of course, the semblance of truth (i.e. falsehood), but the semblance of knowledge (i.e. the δοξαστικὴ ἐπιστήμη of 233C10). It is this unreal and apparent knowledge which induces the thinking or stating of what in some sense is not. To this the Sophist will object (241A–B) that it has just been agreed that nothing can be said to be without any being at all. Accordingly, the dictum of Parmenides must be attacked in self-defence (241D); and it must at all costs be established beyond question that what is not can have being in some respect (κατά τι) and that what is can somehow (πῃ) not be. If this cannot be established, then it will be impossible to speak of false judgements or statements as likenesses or images or copies or semblances, or to speak of the arts, such as the Sophist's, connected with these things, for to do so will at once involve self-contradiction (241E). The Stranger and Theaetetus accordingly agree to attempt the refutation of Parmenides' pronouncement (242A–B). The opening move which the Stranger makes, however, is to examine not the nature of what is not but of what is. This discussion runs from 242C to 259D. It falls into two parts. First, the views of previous thinkers, including Parmenides himself, are considered (242C–245E). After this, the dispute between the materialists and the 'Friends of the Forms' is reviewed and discussed (245E–259D). The conclusion of the first part is that Being is not to be assigned only to one thing or concept or one set of things or concepts; and of the second that Being is to be assigned not only to what is unchanging but also to what is in a state of change.

THE DISCUSSION OF REALITY: PREVIOUS THINKERS

It is not clear to what extent Plato in the first part of the discussion of reality purports to be giving a historical review of the doctrines of previous philosophers. However, the purpose which he intends his argument to serve seems fairly clear from the remarks made by the Stranger at the conclusion of the passage (245 D–E). From these it would appear that Plato is well aware that he has not given an exhaustive account of previous (or possible) definitions of τὸ ὄν. But he appears to feel that the arguments he has given are adequate to justify a claim to be able to refute the identification of τὸ ὄν with any other concept or pair of concepts. It is of course quite true that Existence (if it is proper so to translate τὸ ὄν here) cannot be identified with any other concept or pair of concepts; and this section of the *Sophist* is of considerably less philosophical importance than those which follow it. Without, however, discussing the arguments in any great detail, it is still necessary to consider one or two problems which they raise.

In the first place, it seems clear that Plato does not understand the partisans of Hot and Cold or some other such pair to be maintaining that any and only hot or cold things are real things, or that hot things and cold things are the only things that exist. His argument depends on their having asserted that only two things, namely Hot and Cold, can have existence (or reality) properly assigned to them; he does not set out to attack an assertion that 'to be' must be translated in all contexts into either 'to be hot' or 'to be cold' if it is to be legitimately attributed to anything. Thus whatever assimilation we may detect in later arguments between the existential and copulative senses of εἶναι, it seems evident that it is a specifically existential sense which Plato has in mind here. On the other hand, it is difficult to say with confidence how far existence and reality are being equated in the argument. Presumably the historical partisans of Hot and Cold, whoever they were, did not wish to deny existence altogether to everything but Hot and Cold. What they wished to do was to draw the contrast, familiar at all stages in the history of philosophy, between the apparently and the truly real. The only truly real things are Hot and Cold (or, as the case may be, Wet and Dry), and everything else, although it must somehow exist if only to be spoken of, is only an imitation or offspring of these two. Plato's counter-argument, however, is perfectly susceptible of an interpretation whereby it is Existence as such which is under discussion.[1] Only two things exist, Hot and Cold: but either the existence ascribed to them is a third thing, in which case more than two things exist; or existence is equated with one of them only, in which case it cannot be equated with the other; or existence is assigned to both, in which case they together constitute a single thing, namely Existence.

The argument, however, is very briefly stated and accordingly difficult to evaluate. Plato might be bringing an argument against a disjunctive definition as such. But disjunctive definitions may be perfectly acceptable (for instance an Iberian might be defined as a citizen of either Spain or Portugal); and Plato is not considering whether to be means to be (predicatively) hot or cold, but whether to be means to be (identical with) one of the only two existents, namely Hot and Cold (cf. 243 D 8–E 2). Plato, of course, wishes to show that Existence (or Being) is a third thing, different from either Hot or Cold, just as he will later show (250 A–C) that it is different from κίνησις and στάσις.[2] After the brief argument given, the partisans of Hot and Cold are described as having been placed in a situation in which they could be reasonably asked to offer some further enlightenment (244 A–B). No further exposition, however, is offered on their behalf, and Plato presumably thinks that his case against them has been satisfactorily stated. They might, perhaps, wish to say that what they mean is that only physical objects exist and that all physical objects are merely different compounds of the elemental Hot and Cold. But whatever they might or might not wish to say, no one will now seriously wish to deny that Existence should not be identified with either one or both of Hot and Cold or indeed any other pair of opposites. It therefore seems sensible to proceed without further comment to the next series of arguments.

The Stranger next turns (244 B–D) to the criticism of those who assert that there is only one thing (244 B 9–10 ἕν πού φατε μόνον

---

[1] Cornford (pp. 216–20) has no hesitation in taking the argument to be considering Reality, as opposed to Existence. But Hot and Cold are nowhere said to be ὄντως ὄντα as opposed to everything else which is only partially real; and Cornford's translation of εἶναι at 243 D 9 as 'really are' is not warranted by anything in the text. The fact that Plato did not emancipate himself from equating reality and existence does not prevent the argument from being an attack on the attempt to identify Existence (of any or all degrees) with any pair of concepts.

[2] I offer no translation of these until after a consideration of the merits of different alternatives.

εἶναι). It is difficult to see how this can be interpreted in any but the existential sense of εἶναι; and the assertion under discussion is accordingly that only one thing exists. This is first refuted by a somewhat curious argument. The Stranger argues that this one existent must have two names, 'one' and 'existent', but that this is absurd, if the existence of only one thing has been posited. Now if Plato is arguing that one thing cannot properly be assigned two names, then he is confusing attribution and identity; if, for example, I say that Joe Smith alias Bill Brown is in cell no. 23, I am not saying that there is more than one person in cell no. 23. It is possible that he is guilty of this confusion, although he later on in the *Sophist* shows his awareness of the difference; greater inconsistencies than this have been written within the covers of a single work of philosophy. But two other interpretations are possible. First, Plato could be making the point that a name is something other than its nominee and that there must be therefore three things in the universe, the one real thing and its two names. This point, however, is equally valid whether the thing has two names or one; and it is precisely this point which is made by the Stranger in his immediately following remarks. This interpretation seems therefore to be ruled out. However, the second remaining alternative is feasible. It is to be noticed that the crucial sentence (244 C 8–9) does not explicitly say that it is ridiculous to give two names to the one real thing. It says only that it is ridiculous to say that two names exist. Thus Plato need be saying no more than that for those who say that there is only one thing in the universe it is ridiculous to say that there can be two of anything, whether names or anything else. This interpretation gives perfectly good sense to the argument without committing Plato to a confusion of identity and attribution.[1] The argument then proceeds to show that even one name must be inadmissible to the advocates of a one-thing

---

[1] This confusion is attributed to Plato here by Robinson in his article on 'Plato's *Parmenides*' (*Classical Philology* XXXVII (1942), p. 163). This view I used formerly to share. But Robinson offers no argument in support of it, and I am satisfied that the interpretation here offered is more likely to be correct. Robinson also cites *Soph.* 250 as an instance of this confusion. This passage will be considered in due course. Cornford's interpretation of 244 B–255 E attributes the confusion to Plato because Cornford maintains (pp. 220–1) that Plato is assuming his own doctrine that names have meanings and meanings are Forms. In fact, of course, Plato need not be assuming anything of the kind; and Cornford is driven to the expedient we saw him adopt in the *Theaetetus* of saying that 'the argument is somewhat disguised by the Stranger's avoiding the mention of Forms' (p. 221). For Plato's awareness that the same thing may possibly have more than one name, cf. *Prot.* 349 B.

universe. For either the name is different from the thing, in which case there are two things; or the name is the same as the thing, in which case it cannot name it.

The Stranger then proceeds to criticize the conception of this one real thing (244 D–245 E). This argument is considerably more complex. It recalls and indeed reproduces some of the argumentation of the second part of the *Parmenides*, and its purpose is to show that the one real thing is not Unity or Wholeness and therefore that more than one thing exists. The further effect of this is to show that Existence cannot be equated with either Unity or Wholeness. Since, again, this is something which no one would be seriously disposed to argue, it does not seem necessary to offer a detailed analysis of the argument. The Stranger, as we have already remarked, concludes with the observation (245 D–E) that countless other difficulties of immeasurable perplexity will arise for anyone who maintains that Existence is to be identified with any one or two things. He has not, of course, gone through an exhaustive list of all possible candidates, but he expresses a justifiable confidence that he has given grounds for a claim to be able to dispose of whatever others might be put forward. Before leaving the argument, however, there is one further difficulty which should not be passed over without comment. Parts of the argument of 242 C to 245 E can, as we have remarked, be interpreted as showing that Existence is not to be equated with any other concept or pair of concepts. But the argument is not only about what Existence is but also about what things exist. Plato could, if he wished, have drawn a clear distinction between the two by speaking of Existence as οὐσία or τὸ εἶναι and by using τὸ ὄν to mean only 'what there is'. In fact, however, he does not make any such clear distinction. This point is of some importance. No detailed examination of the arguments of this section has been offered since its conclusions are the least interesting of any in the *Sophist*. But it should be noticed that although Plato is certainly talking about Existence, he does not explicitly distinguish the question 'what is Existence?' from the question 'what exists?'

This does not, of course, mean that we are back in the throes of the problem of self-predication. It is not illegitimate (indeed it is trivial) to say that Existence is existent, although it is illegitimate to say that unpunctuality is unpunctual or that triangularity is a triangle. But because of Plato's failure to distinguish clearly between the questions of what existence is and of what exists, there is at least the suspicion of a confusion of identity and attribution, as, for instance, at 243E8 (in the attack on the proponents of Hot and Cold) and at 245B7-9 (in the criticism of Parmenides). The trouble is that although the conclusions of these arguments are unexceptionable, there seems no way of being certain exactly what Plato thought he was doing in them. It has seemed safe to suggest that he was consciously arguing both that more than one or two things exist and that Existence itself cannot be equated with any other concept. But it cannot plausibly be claimed that he is giving a specific and unequivocal discussion of the concept of Existence as such. This point is of importance in considering the subsequent discussion of the nature of Being. Plato, although he has argued that we cannot legitimately say of anything that it has no existence whatever, does not discuss what exactly we mean when we say that something exists. Nor does he consider whether existence is a predicate, although he appears (if he can be said at all to be dealing with it as such) to treat it as one. Here again, he (and his commentators) are bedevilled by his language. As τὸ καλόν is natural Greek for 'beauty'[1] so τὸ ὄν is natural Greek for 'existence'. But this terminology inherently involves a confusion between what has Being and what Being is. Moreover, as was pointed out in the discussion of flux in the *Theaetetus*, ὄν for Plato does duty for 'real' as well as 'existent' not only in the middle dialogues and (whenever it belongs) the *Timaeus*, but also in the *Laws*[2] and in the *Sophist* itself.[3] In this capacity, it is of course a predicate; and since for Plato the two capacities coalesce and can be spoken of as a matter of degree, it is of course natural to use them predicatively. There is nowhere in Plato a discussion which we can call without qualification a discussion of what we ourselves understand by existence.[4] Perhaps the most significant point to emphasize in considering this question is that

---

[1] On the Greek and, in particular, Platonic use of the neuter adjective and article, see Bluck (1), pp. 175-8. Hence, of course, self-predication.

[2] *Laws* 894A (see p. 23, n. 1); cf. 894C (where the point is not that μεταβολή and κίνησις exist, for they must have existence of some kind; it is that they are *real* things, i.e. supremely existent).

[3] *Soph.* 266E1.

[4] This, of course, is not to say that there is agreement about existence among all contemporary philosophers. See, for example, G. Nakhnikian and W. C. Salmon, '"Exists" as a Predicate', *Philosophical Review* LXVI (1957), pp. 535-42; also the articles cited in p. 66, n. 1. But there is agreement among all these philosophers about the subject of dispute, which could not be said to include Plato.

Plato does not have a separate Form for Existence; for as has already been pointed out his οὐσία (or τὸ εἶναι or τὸ ὄν) has to do duty for the copulative as well as the existential functions of the verb 'to be'. This is not yet to say that for Plato 'to be' only had meaning where 'to be' is to be *x* or *y*. But it is to say that Plato never evolved or adopted a systematic use of language for the discussion of existence as such.

THE DISCUSSION OF REALITY: MATERIALISM, IDEALISM AND CHANGE

At the conclusion of his argument against those who identify τὸ ὄν with a single thing or pair of things, the Stranger turns to those who discuss the matter in a different way (245 E).[1] This prefatory remark introduces the 'battle of gods and giants' between the materialists, who assert that only what is corporeal truly exists, and the idealists, who assert that true existence (or reality) resides only in bodiless Forms (246 A–249 D). Much has been written in the attempt to establish an identification for the 'Friends of the Forms'. But such an identification, even if successfully vindicated against the rest, would not contribute any further clarification of the argument itself; indeed, it is the interpretation of the argument itself which must provide the most cogent grounds for the acceptance or rejection of any particular identification. The most plausible identification is perhaps that whereby the 'Friends of the Forms' are members of the Academy who had over-emphasized the dichotomy of γένεσις and οὐσία which finds expression in the earlier dialogues. But no certain identification is possible.[2] More important to notice is the language in which the dispute between the materialists and the idealists is first outlined (246 A–C). From it we can derive further evidence for Plato's retention

[1] Cornford (p. 228, n. 1) rightly argues against any attempt to interpret this phrase unnaturally in the interests of some theory as to the identity of the 'Friends of the Forms'. Cf. Campbell *ad loc.* citing *Crat.* 425 A.

[2] Ross (pp. 105–7) gives a concise summary of the different views that have been held. His own preference is for Plato's earlier self. But although the *Sophist* may be regarded as modifying the χωρισμός of the *Phaedo*, the disjunction between γένεσις and οὐσία was, as we have noticed, never absolute, even in the *Phaedo* itself. Moreover, the language used suggests a group of contemporaries; and the Stranger's διὰ συνήθειαν (248 B 8) is more natural on this interpretation. The view which I have adopted is close to that adopted by Cherniss ((3), p. 80). But Cherniss is inclined to his view by a unitarian interpretation of Plato which I cannot accept, and his interpretation of Plato's discussion of the 'Friends' is, as will be seen, incompatible with my own.

of his gradational ontology and his equation of true existence and reality, for he criticizes neither party on the grounds that everything must exist (i.e. that nothing, as earlier shown, can be assigned to the class of τὰ μηδαμῶς ὄντα); on the contrary, he makes it plain that the issue is as to which of the contents of the universe merits the ascription of true reality (ἀληθινὴν οὐσίαν 246Β8). Thus εἶναι here (as at 246Α10) means not 'to have some sort of being' (i.e. to exist, or εἶναί πως), but 'to have *real* being'. The materialists do not deny the existence of souls, they assert only that souls are corporeal (247Β8); and the idealists do not deny existence to the phenomenal world, they only refuse to allow it more than the partial reality of γένεσις (248Α). The dispute is not one concerning existence; but it is the verb εἶναι and its derivatives which are used, none the less, and which are treated throughout as susceptible of degree.

The Stranger's argument against the materialists is straightforward. They admit the existence of mind, and that one mind (or soul) may be just and another unjust. They think that mind is in fact corporeal; but they cannot venture to assert that the justice which can be present in individual minds is corporeal (or altogether non-existent). After thus driving them to accept the reality of some bodiless entities, at least, the Stranger offers for their acceptance a criterion (ὅρος) of reality. This criterion is the capacity to affect or be affected by something else.[1]

Commentators have been much exercised as to whether Plato is here putting forward a definition of reality of his own.[2] But as Cornford[3] rightly points out, it is in any case something more like a symptom than a definition which seems to be meant. Plato appears to have in mind the argument made familiar in the earlier exposition and development of the Theory of Forms. The existence of such qualities (or, for Plato, entities) as goodness or whiteness or beauty must be inferred

[1] The sentence τίθεμαι γὰρ ὅρον ὁρίζειν τὰ ὄντα ὡς ἔστιν οὐκ ἄλλο τι πλὴν δύναμις (247Ε3–4) has troubled editors. It is generally agreed that the criterion, not τὰ ὄντα, should be nothing other than δύναμις, but this reading is felt to be indefensible as the text stands (thus Cornford, p. 234, n. 1). Ast proposes to delete ὁρίζειν, Badham to delete ὁρίζειν τὰ ὄντα. But I cannot see why the text as it stands cannot be so read as to yield the desired meaning, although it cannot be denied that the most immediately natural interpretation is to take δύναμις as referring to τὰ ὄντα.

[2] In favour of this view, see e.g. Lutoslawski, p. 423; Ritter, *op. cit.* pp. 170–4. Against, Taylor, *op. cit.* p. 384; Cornford, pp. 238–9.

[3] Cornford, p. 238, n. 3. I have elsewhere, in discussing the *Parmenides*, attempted to point out some of the difficulties attached to the translation of ὁρίζειν (or ὁρίζεσθαι) as used by Plato.

from their visible effects, that is to say, their perceptible presence in the phenomenal particulars of this world. Thus white hairs are white because of the presence of whiteness (*Lysis* 217D), good men are good because of the presence of goodness (*Gorg.* 498D) and beautiful colours or shapes are beautiful because of the presence of beauty (*Phaedo* 100D). Thus here the materialists, since they admit that souls can be just, are admitting the presence in souls of justice; therefore they must admit that justice, whose discernible effect they acknowledge, is itself a real thing. Whether such incorporeal entities as justice possess the capacity to be acted upon as well as to act upon other things is not explicitly discussed in the argument against the materialists. It becomes of crucial importance, however, in the argument against the 'Friends of the Forms'.

This argument has proved the source of much contention. According to what may be regarded as the orthodox view,[1] Plato is here doing no more than establishing that change itself and changing souls[2] must be included among what is truly real. But this view, although it fits that part of the argument which runs from 248E6 to 249B3,[3] involves the explaining away of 248A4–E5. This previous section shows that the idealists, who allow the capacity to affect and be affected by something else to the phenomenal world, must allow it also to the real world. For they allow that the real world can be known; but they have to deny that to know something is to act upon something and that to be known is to be acted upon if they are to maintain that the real world is altogether changeless. The orthodox interpreters of this section of the argument are forced to maintain that Plato shared with the idealists a view that being known is not being acted upon. But this makes it very hard to see what can then be the point of Plato's introducing the argument (based on his own proposed criterion of reality) at all. To say, for instance, with Ross[4] that the suggestion that to be known is to be acted on 'is silently dropped when the consequence of accepting it

---

[1] Cornford, pp. 245–8; Ross, pp. 110–11; Cherniss (6), pp. 238–9. Against, Owen (1), p. 85, n. 2, citing this passage as evidence for Plato's jettisoning his earlier disjunction of γένεσις and οὐσία. Owen does not, however, offer any arguments in support of his view of this passage.

[2] *Laws* 896E–897A, 966D–E.

[3] This passage has sometimes been taken to show that Plato assigns life and soul to the Forms. But this is not only highly improbable and quite unsupported elsewhere, but is in no way required by the text, which asserts only that reality *includes* both life and soul.

[4] Ross, p. 111.

has been pointed out' fails to explain either why Plato does not believe that to be known is to be acted upon or why, if he agrees with the idealists in the first place, he thinks it necessary that the suggestion should be put to them. Plato does, of course, conclude his whole argument by saying that if everything is in flux (249 B 8 φερόμενα καὶ κινούμενα) then knowledge is impossible, for the objects of knowledge must be stable (249 B κατὰ ταὐτὰ καὶ ὡσαύτως καὶ περὶ τὸ αὐτό). But he does not say that this makes it false to assert that a stable Form F is different in some sense when known by X at time t from when not so known.

The issues raised here are of sufficient importance to call for a digression from the exegesis of the immediate argument.[1] In considering Plato's treatment of flux in the *Cratylus* and *Theaetetus*, we have already seen that although he did not believe that the perceptible world is in fact in a state of constant and total change, he believed that but for the Forms it would be. This view we can reinterpret without undue distortion by saying that he saw that ostensive reference can only be fixed by the imputation or detection of some qualitative identity. In fact, Plato is here a little near to Hume, for like Hume he is well aware that imputation of identity may be an error. What grounds do we have that entitle us to assume either that Thursday's objects are Wednesday's objects or that Thursday's observer is Wednesday's observer? The answer, of course, is the discernible presence of permanent characteristics. We can see what the Cratyleans meant by their assertion that one cannot step into the same river even once. But one can step into as many different river stages of the same river process as one chooses; and, as Quine points out, it is the identification of the different rivers which determines our subject-matter to be a river process and not a river stage. This vindication of ostension may lead in turn to a recognition of the difference between identity and attribution. To take Quine's example again, we come to see the difference between pointing to a river and saying 'Caÿster' and pointing to a square object and saying 'square'. We see, in fact, the difference between instances of an abstract universal and parts of a physical whole.

But at this point we are already beyond the valid interpretation of Plato. For although Plato distinguishes in the *Sophist* between identity

[1] The remarks that follow are in part prompted by Quine's discussion of identity, ostension and hypostasis, *op. cit.* pp. 65 ff.

and attribution, he does so in a very different context; and although he shows in the *Parmenides* that the relation of particulars to Forms is not that of parts to physical wholes, he never does establish what the relation is. Moreover, the problem is seen by Plato in terms of his own gradational ontology. For him, those things that are least liable to change are those that most truly exist, and are most truly knowable. Thus in the *Philebus* the truest knowledge is said to be that which is περὶ τὸ ὂν καὶ τὸ ὄντως καὶ τὸ κατὰ ταὐτὸν ἀεὶ πεφυκός (58 A). Similarly, it is reasserted at 61 D–E that knowledge of those things that are liable to change (τὰ γιγνόμενα καὶ ἀπολλύμενα) is less true than that of those whose qualities are permanent and immutable. To sensitive logical nostrils there is here a residual whiff of self-predication. Phenomenal things cannot be truly known because their properties (derived from Forms) are impermanently exemplified and they are accordingly subject to the μεταβολὴ εἰς ἄλλην ἕξιν of *Laws* 894 A.[1] But the Forms themselves are unchanging; that is to say, the properties which they possess are not only unalloyed but indestructible. Now it is not made explicit what these properties are; and (with the possible exception of *Soph.* 258 B–C) there is no explicit statement of self-predication in the late dialogues. But there remains a suspicion that Plato still regarded the Forms as the permanent possessors of those same qualities which can only temporarily and partially be exemplified in particulars, and that they were still, for him, the repositories and exemplifications of the same beauty and whiteness and hardness which endow the things of this world with their fleeting identity.

This last consideration, however, must remain uncertain, for Plato never specifies just what qualities he is prepared to ascribe to the Forms after the criticisms brought against them in the *Parmenides*.[2] His concern is more to determine their interrelations than to describe their properties; and the *Philebus* fails to fulfil its apparent promise of a discussion of the nature of the Forms (15 B). But what is without question certain is that in the *Sophist* Plato allows that change of some kind is perfectly compatible with real existence. More than this, in the last book of the *Laws* Plato asserts that it is precisely by κίνησις that the

---

[1] See p. 23, n. 1.

[2] As stated in the Introduction, I do not propose to cite evidence on this question from the *Timaeus* since its orthodox dating must be regarded as not beyond suspicion.

soul is given its eternal existence.[1] On the other hand, it is equally certain that there is change of some kind from which the objects of knowledge must be altogether exempt. The difficulty, therefore, if we are to understand the argument against the 'Friends of the Forms', is to establish what sort of change is being talked about.

Unfortunately, Plato nowhere draws a clear distinction (as Aristotle does in the *De Generatione et Corruptione*) between spatial movement, quantitative change, qualitative change and total loss of identity. In the *Theaetetus* he distinguishes spatial movement from qualitative change (181 c–d). But the ten kinds of κίνησις distinguished in *Laws* 893 b ff. complicate rather than clarify the more important distinctions. However, in the *Theaetetus* the argument against the partisans of flux demonstrates that their position is absurd since it denies meaning to any word of ostensive significance. That is to say, despite the fact of phenomenal change the ascription of some sort of existence and identity to the things of this world is legitimate. But Plato does not, of course, deny the fact of phenomenal change, except to the world of Forms. This, as we have seen, appears to mean that the Forms, unlike the things of this world, are the possessors of immutable characteristics. Now whatever these immutable characteristics are, they are not rendered any less immutable by the fact of being known. If X comes to know unitary Form F on Tuesday, it does not become any less unitary than it was on Monday. Indeed, it will never cease to be unitary in the way that a garment, for instance (to take an example from the *Phaedo*), must by the process of time one day lose its unitary identity. But there is obviously a sense in which a known-by-X Form can be said to be different from a not-known-by-X Form. The permanent characteristics which make it what it is are unchanged. But it is now both affecting and being affected by the mind of X who knows it.

Thus there appears to be a plausible sense in which Plato can have thought that the Forms can change without forfeiting their changelessness. They can, in fact, be truly known without thereby forfeiting the immutable identity without which they could not be susceptible of being truly known; and it is thus that they exhibit the hallmark of reality, the capacity to affect, and be affected. It is difficult to deny that this δύναμις argument is made centrally relevant both to the argument against the materialists and to that against the idealists. In the first

---

[1] *Laws*, 966 d–e.

argument, as we saw, it is not made explicit that justice and the rest are being known and therefore affected. But the second argument would seem to show that this also is meant. For it is because the materialists must admit that they can detect justice in individual souls that they are driven to acknowledge its existence. Justice is knowable by its presence. In other words, justice affects other things by being present in them, and is affected by being thereby known.

There is a further point which Plato may have had in mind. The knowing of F by X is an event in time; and to say that F affects or is affected by something in the phenomenal world is to speak of a datable event. Thus if Forms can be the subject-matter of datable events, they can be thereby treated in time; and if Form F is known by X on Monday and Y on Tuesday, it is a day older when known by Y than when known by X. The question of whether a Form can be said to grow older than itself is one of the many topics discussed in the second part of the *Parmenides*;[1] and growing older is classified in the *Theaetetus* among the examples of qualitative change (181 D 1). However, the fact is that Plato does not, in the *Sophist*, follow up his argument along these lines, and the *Parmenides* cannot be taken as evidence that he ever drew any such conclusions as have been outlined above. He seems only concerned to show that what is truly real can be subject (and indeed must be) to the affection of knowledge without forfeiting the unchangeability of its permanent characteristics. Moreover—and about this conclusion of the argument there is no dispute among commentators—he asserts the true reality of mind (or soul) although it must of its very nature be subject to κίνησις. The final conclusion is stated at 249 C–D. The philosopher must adopt an intermediate position between the partisans of changelessness (Parmenides and the 'Friends of the Forms') and the partisans of total flux.[2] He must admit that reality includes things both unchangeable and in change (249 D 3 ὅσα ἀκίνητα καὶ κεκινημένα).

---

[1] *Parm.* 152 A–155 C. The conclusion reached is that Unity both is and is becoming older and younger than itself and everything else, and also that it is not and is not becoming either older or younger than itself or everything else.

[2] Cf. *Theaet.* 180 C–181 B where the two sides (Parmenides and the Heracliteans) are reviewed, and Socrates concludes with the ironical comment that if both sides turn out to be saying nothing reasonable (μέτριον) 'we shall be absurdly foolish if we suppose that insignificant people like ourselves can contribute anything to the discussion, after disqualifying these venerable and all-wise men'.

THE μέγιστα γένη AND THE SENSES OF εἶναι

After reaching this conclusion, the Stranger first observes that the question of reality seems to have been satisfactorily dealt with. But he then points out that it is still necessary to undertake such a clarification of terms as was earlier asked of the partisans of Hot and Cold (249D–250A). This leads into a discussion of the terms κίνησις, στάσις and τὸ ὄν, and to the consideration of whether they are all names of separate entities. This leads in turn to the question of combination between them, and from there to the relations between these three and the two further terms ταὐτόν and ἕτερον which the consideration of the original question has introduced into the discussion. The section of the *Sophist* in which Plato considers the interrelations of the μέγιστα γένη is sometimes taken by commentators[1] as beginning only at 251 A with the statement of the question how one thing can have several names. But although the previous remark of the Stranger (250E) implies that what has gone before is only the statement of the problem, the argument from 250A to c is important to the development of the subsequent argument. Accordingly the discussion of the μέγιστα γένη should properly be regarded as running from 250A8 to 259D8.

Before turning to the argument, however, the question of translation requires to be dealt with. The dangers of translating τὸ ὄν as 'Existence' rather than 'Being' have already been pointed out. But the other four kinds also raise problems of their own. For τὸ ταὐτόν and τὸ ἕτερον 'Identity' and 'Difference' are perhaps preferable to 'Sameness' and 'Otherness', for the word 'sameness' in English tends to imply want of variety rather than the more logical overtones here required. More difficult is to find an appropriate translation of κίνησις and στάσις. The accepted rendering, established by Cornford, is 'Motion' and 'Rest'. But it is change as well as motion which is meant by κίνησις, and it is as 'change' that it is translated by Cornford himself during the previous discussion. 'Change' would certainly seem to be the better rendering where both spatial movement and qualitative change is meant,[2] for change can more readily carry the overtone of motion (as in 'change of place') than *vice versa* (thus 'qualitative motion' is absurd). But there is no English word which conveys the notion of lack both of movement and of change. 'Rest', although it does not in English suggest a very

---

[1] Thus Cornford and Ackrill (2).   [2] Cf. *Theaet.* 181B–182A.

important or pervasive concept in the structure (whether physical or logical) of the world, is perhaps still the most feasible of any possible alternatives. Accordingly, the five kinds will be rendered in the discussion which follows as Being, Change, Rest, Identity and Difference.

It does not seem necessary to follow through the whole of this much-discussed passage in detail, for some, at least, of its conclusions may be safely summarized without argument. Thus it may be accepted without citing further support from the text that Plato gives both a description and a demonstration of the philosopher's task in assessing the inter-relations between Forms. He distinguishes five particularly important Forms of which the first three (Being, Change and Rest) have already proved central to much of the previous discussion; and discussion of these first three leads almost at once to the introduction of the two further Forms of Identity and Difference. In the course of establishing the relations between these five, Plato shows how the dictum of Parmenides may be circumvented. The claim is satisfactorily vindicated that blending or combination of some kind is possible between the different Forms, and it is asserted that it is by this combination of Forms that discourse (λόγος) is enabled to take place at all. This brief outline requires no further comment. But three important and difficult questions are raised by the closer analysis of the argument, and these require to be considered in greater detail. The first is whether Plato at all distinguished the existential sense of εἶναι as such. The second is his treatment of the copula. The third is his analysis of negation.

That Plato marks off the existential sense of εἶναι from at least one other sense seems to be generally agreed.[1] However, there are grounds (of which some have been already indicated) for holding that this assumption requires at least a degree of modification. In the first place, as previously remarked, Plato does not mark off by name as a Form a sense of εἶναι in which it need not and cannot be provided with a filling of the form 'to be x or y', in either the predicative or identitative sense. This failure to distinguish the existential sense as such is clearly demonstrated by the argument of 256 D 12–E6, which runs as follows:

STR. For the nature of Difference makes each one of all the kinds different from Being (τὸ ὄν) and therefore something that is not (οὐκ ὄν); and on this principle we shall be right in speaking of all of them as things which in this sense 'are not' (οὐκ ὄντα), and also as things which, since

E

[1] Cornford, p. 296; Ackrill (2), p. 1.

they partake in Being (μετέχει τοῦ ὄντος), have being and are (εἶναί τε καὶ ὄντα).

TH. So it seems.

5 STR. So about each of the Forms there is much that it is and a countless number of things that it is not.

This passage is taken by both Cornford[1] and Ackrill[2] to be referring at 256 E 3 to the existential sense of εἶναι. But that the phrase μετέχει τοῦ ὄντος cannot here be the philosopher's formulation of the existential use is shown by the Stranger's next remark. For this makes it clear that it is the copulative sense which is covered by the phrase. The Stranger would be talking nonsense if he said that for each one of the Forms 'there are many things that it exists' or 'it is existence in many respects'. It is in any case not the existence of the Forms which requires to be demonstrated, but the fact that they can both be and not be in the copulative sense. What the Stranger goes on to say (257 A) is that Being (τὸ ὄν) must therefore be marked off from the other kinds. This is translated by Cornford 'Existence'. But from the previous sentence it is clear that this is not existence but the Being which each of the Forms can be in many respects. In fact, throughout the discussion there is an assimilation to each other of the existential and copulative senses.

In the second place, it must be noticed that Plato explicitly suggests at 250 E–251 A that the problems of Being and non-Being parallel each other. The Stranger remarks that both are equally puzzling and that any light thrown on the one will serve likewise to illuminate the other. Now what in fact happens is that no solution is offered for the dilemma of 237–9, where it was shown that what has no being whatever cannot be dealt with or even spoken of at all. What Plato does is to show that statements of the form 'so-and-so is not x, y, etc.' can be satisfactorily vindicated in the face of Parmenides' dictum. If we are meant to draw from this a parallel solution to the problems of Being, then we should presumably conclude that the question of Being without a filling (that is to say, Being in the purely existential sense) is to be disregarded on the grounds of being capable of circumvention but not of solution. Indeed, it is in fact the case that Plato does not consider the problem

---

[1] Cornford, p. 288.

[2] Ackrill, p. 1 'μετέχει τοῦ ὄντος is the philosopher's equivalent of the existential ἔστιν; but as will be seen, it is not his analysis of ἔστιν in its other uses. So the existential meaning is marked off.'

of existence as such. He establishes only that everything must have some sort of Being; but this cannot be said to be the same thing.

Against this, however, must be set both the sections of the argument earlier in the dialogue where, as we have seen, Plato does appear to be talking about existence, and also those passages in which he uses εἶναι when it is clear that no filling is either needed or intended. In some cases, it is by no means certain whether such a use is not in fact incomplete because promissory; thus at 256 A 1, when the phrase μετέχειν τοῦ ὄντος is taken up, it is not existentially. But in two places the purely existential sense does appear to be what is meant. In both (250 A 11 and 254 D 10) the point being made is that Change, Rest and Being are three distinct and separate kinds, of which both the first two can stand in a relation to the third. In fact, it is because we say that Change and Rest both have Being (but do not mean by this either that both change or both rest) that we must conclude that Being is itself a third and separate Form. Here, it is clear, Plato does not mean that Change and Rest 'are' in any sense that requires a filling (whether of identity or predication), for he is concerned only with the three separate notions of Being, Rest and Change. His argument depends on the legitimacy of the assertions κίνησις ἔστιν and στάσις ἔστιν irrespective of what else there may be which it is legitimate to assert that κίνησις or στάσις are. It would accordingly seem that in two passages at least (although it is the same argument being put forward in both cases) Plato is deliberately using εἶναι in a sense where it is legitimate and complete without the addition of anything to convert it into an identitative or copulative use.

The conclusion, then, must be that although Plato did not believe that εἶναι could only be legitimately used where 'to be' means 'to be something', he still did not specifically distinguish the existential sense as such. Indeed, he more accurately distinguishes the negative existential sense from those of negative identity and negative predication, for he sees that he can deal with statements of the form 'X is not such-and-such' but cannot deal with 'X is not' (i.e. ἔστι μηδαμῶς ὄν) in the (existential) sense where it has no filling. Moreover, his analysis of false statement depends precisely upon his awareness that such a statement is not required to bear non-existential import. Because, as we shall see, he is in the *Sophist* emancipated from the atomistic model on which all words are the names of things in the universe, he is able to see that to say something that is not the case is not to name something that does not exist. His awareness of the problems of non-existence might tend to suggest that he must also have been aware of the problems of existence. But although he shows that since total lack of being is impossible everything must have being of some kind, he does not distinguish a sense of being for which no filling can be supplied and which requires to be explicity marked off from the copula or the identity-sign.

It is not impossible (although he does not himself say this) that Plato did think that for all legitimate uses of Being a filling could be supplied, just as it must be possible to supply a filling if non-Being is to be legitimately spoken of. He certainly seems to think that it is true to say both that whatever is is the same as itself[1] and that whatever is is in some sense one.[2] Thus he may have thought that such a phrase as κίνησις ἔστιν is legitimate as it stands because it can be taken as entailing that (at the least) κίνησις is single and the same as itself, whereas to say that κίνησις ἔστι μηδαμῶς ὄν is absurd. If this is so, then we should have grounds for arguing that Plato's assimilation of the existential and copulative senses of εἶναι amounts virtually to the obliteration of the difference. But he in fact appears to think that κίνησις μετέχει τοῦ ὄντος is a valid statement on its own, for although when it is taken up in 256A this is not, as we have remarked, in the existential sense, it would appear to be one of the statements about the five kinds introduced in 255E, and as such to require no further addition or translation. Plato does not, it is true, translate κίνησις ἕτερον ταὐτοῦ ἔστιν into κίνησις μετέχει τοῦ ἑτέρου πρὸς ταὐτόν and thus he may mean by κίνησις μετέχει τοῦ ὄντος that Change partakes in the specifically relational (i.e. copulative) Being of the Stranger's immediately following remark. But it seems more probable that he is asserting at 256A1 (as at 250A11 and 254D10) a valid relation between two of the five kinds in a context where no further concept requires to be introduced in order to establish the validity of the relation. If this is so, then he is certainly using εἶναι in what we cannot call anything other than the existential sense. But this is still not to say that he gave specific recognition to the concept of existence as such. The conclusion must remain that even if he saw that the properties of the Form of Being are such that 'X partakes of

---

[1] *Soph.* 256A7–8 Ἀλλὰ μὴν αὕτη γ' ἦν ταὐτὸν διὰ τὸ μετέχειν αὖ πάντ' αὐτοῦ.

[2] *Soph.* 245D4–6 Τὸ γενόμενον ἀεὶ γέγονεν ὅλον· ὥστε οὔτε οὐσίαν οὔτε γένεσιν ὡς οὖσαν δεῖ προσαγορεύειν [τὸ ἓν ἢ] τὸ ὅλον ἐν τοῖς οὖσι μὴ τιθέντα.

Being' is valid without the explicit or tacit appendix that 'X partakes of Being in relation to such-and-such',[1] we must still modify any un-qualified assertion that Plato distinguished the existential from any or all other senses of 'to be'.

The same difficulty must attach to any assertion that Plato explicitly distinguishes the copula, for he does not set up a Form for it, and it is at best uncertain in what formula he is distinguishing it if he is in fact doing so. A strong argument, however, has recently been put forward by Ackrill[2] for ascribing the distinction to Plato. Ackrill suggests that Plato consciously and deliberately assigns to the verb μετέχειν a role which corresponds to the role of the copula in ordinary language. But examination of Plato's use of μετέχειν in the relevant passage leaves this contention a little more questionable than Ackrill's arguments would suggest. Two passages in particular will require a close and critical inspection. However, it will first be convenient to summarize two arguments, both adopted by Ackrill, which tend strongly to modify Cornford's contention[3] that 'the statement that Plato "has discovered the ambiguity of the copula" is far removed from the facts'.

In the first place, Cornford's view that the relation between Forms is symmetrical must be viewed with grave suspicion. Some, at least, of the relations between Forms are certainly asymmetrical (Ackrill's example is Justice to Virtue); and Plato's analogy with notes and letters certainly suggests that the order in some sense as well as the components must be known to make analysis of the relation possible. The statement κίνησις μετέχει τοῦ ὄντος means that Change is, but it does not also express (although this may in some sense be so) the assertion that Being changes. Nor does κίνησις μετέχει θατέρου πρὸς ταὐτόν mean also that Difference in relation to Identity changes. Finally, Plato's use of two different constructions with κοινωνία and its

---

[1] At 255 C 11–12, where the argument is designed to show that the concept (or Form) of Difference is not identical with that of Being, the Stranger says 'Αλλ' οἶμαί σε συγχωρεῖν τῶν ὄντων τὰ μὲν αὐτὰ καθ' αὑτά, τὰ δὲ πρὸς ἄλλα ἀεὶ λέγεσθαι. This might suggest that by the phrase εἶναι αὐτὸ καθ' αὑτό Plato wished to mark off the existential sense from the others. But it is clear from the context that Plato is not distinguishing senses of εἶναι. He is drawing a distinction between kinds of things that are (ὄντα) in order to show that Being, which covers both, must be non-identical with Difference, which covers only one (unless we can say that anything is different without being different from something else). Indeed, εἶναι αὐτὸ καθ' αὑτό could even be used in support of the argument that 'to be' for Plato must always mean to be something.

[2] Ackrill (2).   [3] Cornford, p. 296.

derivatives[1] would suggest that he made a conscious distinction between the general notion of connectedness (expressed by a dative construction) and some sort of determinate non-symmetrical relation (expressed by a genitive construction).

In the second place, Plato's own argument from 256A10 to B4 explicitly shows how it is legitimate to assert that Change both is and is not ταὐτόν. Change both is (copula) identical with itself and is not (identity-sign) Identity. The possibility of ambiguity, of course, depends in the first place upon the Greek use of ταὐτόν both for 'Identity' and for 'the same thing'. But Plato, in exposing the ambiguity, is distinguishing between two different senses of εἶναι, not between senses of ταὐτόν. The first states an attribution and the second an identity; and when we say that Change is ταὐτόν we are not speaking in the same sense (ὁμοίως) as when we say that it is μὴ ταὐτόν.

These arguments tell strongly against Cornford's position. But there are further considerations which tend to show that the claim that Plato explicitly distinguished the copula requires a certain modification. In the first place, as already pointed out, he does not distinguish the copula as a separate Form, although he distinguishes Identity as a separate Form such that a statement of identity of the form '*X* is *A*' asserts a relation of μέθεξις between *X* and the Form of Identity (in relation to *A*). This suggests an assimilation of the identity-sign to the copula. For just as the statement 'The Prime Minister is a man' states, for Plato, a relation of μέθεξις between the Prime Minister and the Form of Manhood, so the statement 'The Prime Minister is Mr Macmillan' states a relation of μέθεξις between the Prime Minister and the Form of Identity (in relation to the nominee of 'Mr Macmillan'). Applied to the argument of 256A10–B4, this means that Plato explains the difference between κίνησις ἔστι ταὐτόν and κίνησις ἔστι μὴ ταὐτόν not by showing that one asserts a relation of identity and one a relation of attribution, but by showing that despite their similarity of form the two statements assert a relation of μέθεξις (or κοινωνία with the genitive) between κίνησις and two different Forms. We have noticed already the

---

[1] Ackrill (2), p. 5. Ackrill also points out (rightly, I believe) that Dürr, in his interesting attempt to formalize the arguments whereby Plato expounds the intercommunion of Forms, gives too little justification for the precision which he ascribes to the terminology used by Plato. Ackrill does not himself claim to give an exhaustive analysis. But he offers strong grounds for the view that Plato had at least some distinction in mind between the kinds of relation holding between the μέγιστα γένη.

difficulties involved in attributing to Plato the distinct and separate recognition of the existential sense of εἶναι; and it is perhaps only safe to attribute to him a recognition that εἶναι can symbolize the relation of its subject either to the Form denoted by a predicate, or to the Form of Identity in relation to the nominee of some other term (if not the subject itself), or to the Form of Being itself (without the need to specify, for the moment, what it is that the subject is).

Moreover, there are two passages where the way in which μετέχειν is used must cast suspicion on the assertion that Plato wished explicitly to single it out for a role corresponding to that of the copula in ordinary language. In one of these (255 D 4) Ackrill himself admits that μετέχειν is used in an exceptional way. He is right that it does not here stand for the symmetrical 'blending' which Cornford holds to be the only relation subsisting among the μέγιστα γένη. But it cannot here stand for the copula, and Ackrill's claim[1] that 'one passage cannot be allowed to outweigh a dozen others' is no defence on behalf of a claim that Plato wishes consciously to assign a distinct and precise logical role to the verb μετέχειν. The argument of this particular passage is difficult, since τὸ καθ᾽ αὑτό and τὸ πρός τι, which are apparently here regarded as Forms, do not reappear elsewhere in the discussion of the relations between Forms, and their role and properties are nowhere clearly defined. What is clear, however, is that Plato asserts that a relation of μέθεξις holds between Being and both of them, whereas this is not the case with Difference. What this seems to mean, in view of the general purpose of the argument,[2] is that what is different must be πρός τι and not αὑτὸ καθ᾽ αὑτό (and therefore Being is not synonymous with Difference). But Plato surely believed that it is true to say that the Form of Difference is (copula) καθ᾽ αὑτό as well as πρός τι since this is true of all Forms; and thus μετεῖχε at 255 D 4 cannot stand for the copula. What is curious is that Plato's argument seems to depend on the view that Difference (as well as particular different things) is somehow πρός τι in a way different from that in which everything must be πρός τι (since everything is different from everything else). There seems almost to be an odd hang-over of self-predication: Difference is more supremely different than all those things (whether Forms or particulars) that are different from Difference and each other. For the argument seems to be that nothing can be different καθ᾽ αὑτό (i.e. partake of

---

[1] Ackrill (2), p. 6.   [2] See p. 88, n. 1.

Difference which should somehow blend, but cannot, with τὸ καθ' αὑτό), but must always be different πρός τι (i.e. partake of Difference which somehow does blend with τὸ πρός τι). On the other hand, it is possible for things to be καθ' αὑτό (i.e. to partake of Being which somehow blends with τὸ καθ' αὑτό) and also to be πρός τι (i.e. to partake of Being which somehow blends with τὸ πρός τι).

But this attempt to expand the argument even a little must remain very tentative, and may already involve a misunderstanding of what was in Plato's mind. Plato seems to be in some sort of muddle between what is different and the Form of Difference (which is itself, of course, different), but the argument is too briefly expounded for it to be possible to see exactly what he means or what sort of relation it is that he believes to subsist between Being and both τὸ καθ' αὑτό and τὸ πρός τι but not between Difference and both of them.[1] It seems evident that Cornford[2] is wrong in saying that the passage shows that μέθεξις is symmetrical in the case of Forms, for although Being must be partaken of by as well as partake of both τὸ καθ' αὑτό and τὸ πρός τι both must partake of Difference although it is asserted that Difference itself cannot partake of both. On the other hand, it is also evident that however we understand the argument, it tells against the view that Plato means μέθεξις to perform the role of the copula. In fact, Plato could have made his point without bringing in μέθεξις with τὸ καθ' αὑτό and τὸ πρός τι at all, for he could have said that when we assert a relation of μέθεξις between something and Difference we imply a further relation which is not necessarily implied when we assert a relation of μέθεξις between something and Being. This would constitute a quite adequate argument to show that Being and Difference are the names of two separate Forms without positing a relation of μέθεξις between the Form of Being and the Form of τὸ καθ' αὑτό which does not hold between the Form of Difference and the Form of τὸ καθ' αὑτό.[3] Perhaps Plato's difficulty is

---

[1] A further difficulty is raised by the whole question of the attitude of Plato and the Academy to the difference between καθ' αὑτό and πρός τι predicates. Plato here seems to say that Difference is only a πρός τι predicate whereas Being is both, but the two terms bore a wider sense to the Academy than to Aristotle (see Owen (2), pp. 107–10), and the normal Academic contrast was between man, fire or water (cf. *Parm.* 130D; for evidence for the Academy, Owen (2), p. 109, n. 36 cites Hermodorus *ap.* Simpl. *Phys.* 247.30ff., Diog. Laert. III, 108 and Sext. Emp. *adv. Math.* x, 263) and such predicates as beautiful or good.   [2] Cornford, p. 281, n. 2.

[3] Plato does not in fact say which of τὸ καθ' αὑτό and τὸ πρός τι is partaken of by Being and not by Difference. But it must be τὸ καθ' αὑτό if the argument is not to be rendered

that he cannot clearly formulate the difference between saying 'The concept of Difference is a relative, not an absolute concept' and saying 'The Form of Difference is a relative, not an absolute thing'. This may explain his introduction of τὸ καθ' αὑτό and τὸ πρός τι as Forms. But whatever the reason, the relation which Plato at 255D4 expresses by μετέχειν and which he denies to hold between the Form of Difference and τὸ καθ' αὑτό must be something other than precisely that relation which is expressed in ordinary language by the copula.

The second passage in which μετέχειν does not precisely stand for the copula is that in which it occurs at 255B1. However, the interpretation of the force of μετέχειν in this particular context must depend on the answer to the very difficult question of what exactly Plato assumes or demonstrates in all the four passages on the relation between Change and Rest of which that between 255A4 and 255B6 is the fourth. In the first of these (250A8–C5) the argument is designed to show that Being is not identical with Change or Rest. In the second (252D2–13) Theaetetus demonstrates the impossibility of total ἐπικοινωνία between Forms by selecting Change and Rest as his examples. In the third (254D4–12) the argument of 250A8–C5 is recapitulated, and it is reasserted that Being, Change and Rest are three separate Forms.[1] In the fourth, the passage from 255A4 to 255B6, the object of the argument is to show that neither Change nor Rest is identical with either Identity or Difference. All four passages require further comment. But this brief summary of their purpose is a sufficient preliminary to the final passage in which the relation of Change to Rest is discussed. This brief passage (256B6–9), which immediately follows the passage in which Plato shows that it is legitimate to assert that κίνησις both is and is not ταὐτόν, may be translated as follows:

> STR. Then if Change itself did in some way stand in a relation of participation (μεταλαμβάνειν+gen.) towards Rest, there would be nothing out of the way in speaking of it as 'at rest'.

yet more difficult to understand, for its assumption is that things are different by partaking in Difference which does not stand in the (non-copula) relation to τὸ καθ' αὑτό which Being can do; for if it did, this would somehow mean that things could be different without being different from anything.

[1] Cornford (p. 274, n. 1) sees that this is the purpose of this argument and that of 252D. But his failure to draw the conclusion which must follow in relation to 256B6–9 drives him to the desperate expedient of following Heindorf in supposing a lacuna after 256B7 (p. 286, n. 3).

TH. Nothing whatever, if we are to agree that some kinds will and some will not stand in some relation (μείγνυσθαι) towards each other.

Now what this passage appears to assert is something which, apart from any support which may be derived from its context, Plato certainly believed to be true.[1] This must follow from any interpretation of 249 B 8–C 8, and particularly from Cornford's, since he is unwilling to concede that the Forms are not στάσιμος even in so far as they possess the δύναμις of being known. Apart from this, the passage is the direct sequel to that in which statements of attribution (κίνησις ἔστι ταὐτόν) are distinguished from statements of identity (κίνησις ἔστι μὴ ταὐτόν). This would strongly suggest that Plato accordingly wishes to point out the conclusion that Change and Rest, although they cannot stand in a relation of identity to each other, can stand in relation of predication. Since, as we have noticed, the purpose of the previous discussions of Change and Rest has been in each case to show that Change and Rest are not identical with each other, or Being, or Identity or Difference, this last passage should present no difficulty whatever. The difficulty, however, arises by virtue of the fact that two of earlier arguments and perhaps a third appear to assert that Change and Rest are not predicable of each other, and to base arguments of non-identity on this assertion.

This fact is the more surprising since the non-identity of Being and Identity is proved by simple substitution at 255 B 8–C 4. If Being is identical with Identity, then to say that Change or Rest is is to say that Change or Rest is the same. But this is not what we mean when we say that Change or Rest is. Therefore Being and Identity are not one and the same thing. Now Plato could equally well have used this argument to show that Change is not identical with Rest. He could have said that to say that something changes does not mean that it is at rest, therefore Change and Rest are not one and the same thing. But he does not do so; and to attempt to find some answer to this problem we must consider each of the arguments about Change and Rest in turn. The first (250 A 8–C 5), although it precedes the Stranger's statement

---

[1] Cf. 254 B–D where it is said that some Forms can pervade everything. There seems a clear implication (although it is not explicitly stated) that this applies to the μέγιστα γένη. But it must follow from this that they are mutually predicable, or else it would be false to assert that they have the totality of existents as their extension. Cf. 249 D 3–4, 253 B–C.

of the puzzlement which is to be resolved in the subsequent argument, must be considered as a part of this argument since it is the only proof offered that Being is not identical with either Change or Rest. Like the argument of 255B8–C4, it rests on a simple proof by substitution. When we say that both Change and Rest are, we do not mean either that both are changing or that both are standing still. Therefore Being is distinct from Change and Rest. This conclusion is agreed to by Theaetetus and the Stranger at 255C1–4; but unfortunately the Stranger goes on to assert as the apparent consequence of this that Being is according to its own nature neither changing nor standing still. Now it seems clear from the Stranger's following remarks that it is precisely this apparent consequence of the argument which constitutes the puzzle which the discussion of the interrelations between the μέγιστα γένη is going to solve; and it is precisely by the analysis of the nature of Identity and the ambiguity of εἶναι that the difference between statements of identity and attribution is elucidated. Thus the most plausible way to take the Stranger's erroneous deduction from the preceding argument is as Plato's conscious statement of an unreal difficulty which (against the late learners[1] of 251A–C) is duly to be resolved. This statement of puzzlement by the Stranger is also the passage which, as we have noticed, must modify the assumption that Plato distinguishes the existential sense of εἶναι, for it clearly implies that the solutions of Being and non-Being will parallel each other. What Plato proceeds to do is to show how 'is not' may be translated into 'is different from' and how 'is' may stand either for 'partakes of identity with' or 'partakes of' in the predicative sense. Thus a perfectly plausible way to understand the first discussion of Change and Rest is as a valid proof of the non-identity of Being with either, followed by the statement of an apparent difficulty which the subsequent discussion will resolve.

The second passage (252D2–13), however, is more difficult to interpret in this light. The reason given why the suggestion can be rejected

---

[1] The reference to the 'elderly people whose poverty of intelligence leads them to be astonished at such things' is generally taken to be directed against Antisthenes (see p. 18, n. 2), although the evidence of Aristotle is too slender and cursory to make this certain and Diogenes Laertius says nothing which entitles us to ascribe to Antisthenes the specific confusion ascribed by Plato to the late learners. This confusion is certainly that between identity and predication, but the language of *Soph.* 251A–C could also cover a denial by the late learners of such a general aggregation of ὀνόματα as produces the complexes or 'syllables' of Socrates' 'dream' in the *Theaetetus*.

that all the Forms can combine (ἐπικοινωνία + dat. at 252D3, ἐπιγίγνεσ-θαι at D7) with each other is that this would entail the impossible conclusion that 'Change itself would stand still in all respects (παντά-πασιν) and again Rest itself would be in change'. Now there are two possible and valid arguments by which Plato could maintain that the relation of Change to Rest shows that not all Forms can combine with each other. On the one hand, he could show that they are not identical with each other, and it is not impossible that this is what he had in mind; but if so his argument involves something very like a variant of self-predication. For on this view Plato must somehow feel that it is because Change must be changing and Rest must be at rest that the identity of Change and Rest would entail the absurd conclusion that Change is at Rest and Rest is changing; and accordingly to assert the unchangeability of Rest and the instability of Change is to assert the non-identity of Rest and Change with each other. But if this is so, Plato is (despite his later elucidation of predication and identity) in a considerable muddle. On the other hand, it may be that he means only that Change and Rest are not *entirely* predicable of each other. This interpretation would account for the παντάπασιν of 252D6; and it is important to notice that when the Stranger makes his final observation on the topic at 256B6–7, he secures the assent of Theaetetus only to the suggestion that Change somehow (πη) partakes of Rest. In fact, we have seen from the argument of 248A–249D that Plato believed that all Forms (including, of course, Rest and Change themselves) are both at rest (unchanging), since they are knowable, and changing, since they are known. Thus it is tempting to suggest that at 252D2–13 Plato is showing that total intercommunion between Forms is impossible by citing the example of Change (which is not at a complete standstill) and Rest (which is not in a complete state of change).

This second interpretation, however, is also open to objection. For if this is what Plato is saying, it is on any view a very oblique way of saying it. What he seems to have clearly in mind is to cite two Forms which are by their own nature[1] diametrically opposed to each other in order to show the absurdity of the suggestion that all Forms can super-

---

[1] Thus Change and Rest are originally stated to be diametrically opposed to each other at 250A, and at 255A–B they are said not to blend (μετέχειν) since this would involve their changing to the opposite of their own nature (φύσις). Similarly, everything is said at 255E to be different not by virtue of its own nature (διὰ τὴν αὑτοῦ φύσιν) but by partaking in the Form of Difference.

vene upon each other. Perhaps this should even be regarded as an *ad hominem* argument, since the late learners are people who wish to assimilate all statements to statements of identity. But it seems at any rate difficult to read into the argument as it stands anything that will vindicate Plato against a charge of himself appearing to perpetrate a confusion which it is his object to elucidate. The general purpose of the argument is clear enough, and its point is valid, but perhaps for this very reason it is not very carefully made. The probable conclusion is that Plato may well have had in mind something of both trains of thought which it has been attempted to extract more explicitly from the argument as stated. At this stage of the discussion Plato does not carefully consider the possible analyses of the relation of blending between Change and Rest. It is true both that they are not identical with each other and that they are not entirely predicable of each other. But the assertion that Change can in no sense be said to be at rest and Rest changing Plato certainly believed to be false, and it cannot here be construed as the conscious setting of a puzzle. Accordingly, it seems that at this stage of the discussion Plato has in mind by ἐπι-κοινωνία a sort of total supervention which would involve the commingling of opposite natures and a total mutual predication and identity. It may even be plausible to suggest that at this stage Plato uses statements of the subject–predicate form to state a relation which if analysed would prove to be that of identity. But the argument does not yield to precise dissection; and the most important thing to remark is that its purpose is a very general one, simply to give a readily acceptable example to show that total blending would be absurd.

The third of the four arguments (254D4–12) presents no such problems, and can fortunately be dealt with in far less space. Its purpose is only to reassert that Being, Change and Rest are non-identical with each other; and the word ἀμείκτω at D7 without question expresses a relation of non-identity. No further comment, therefore, is needed except to emphasize that it is the non-identity of Change and Rest which is reasserted without any assertion that mutual predication would be impossible.

We may now turn to the fourth and most important argument (255A4–B4). This argument, unlike the first and third, is directly similar to the second and raises precisely the same difficulty. Indeed, it may even be said that it raises the difficulty more pointedly. For in the second argument, taken by itself, it is impossible to be sure whether it is an argument of non-identity which is at the back of Plato's mind; it may simply be, as we have seen, that he wished to give an obvious example of contrary concepts in order to show that total ἐπικοινωνία (whatever relation or relations the term might cover) was impossible between Forms. In this fourth argument, however, it is certainly non-identity that he has in mind. Yet despite this, he seems to base his argument on the impossibility of mutual predication between Change and Rest. The argument is concise to the point of ellipsis, but it seems to run as follows: Identity and Difference are predicable both of Change and Rest; therefore if either Change or Rest is identical with Identity or Difference, the other of the pair must come to partake of its opposite; but this is impossible; therefore neither Change nor Rest can be identical with either Identity or Difference.

In the face of this difficulty, we are forced to the same conclusion as in the second of the four arguments. Plato cannot mean precisely the copula here by μετέχειν. What he must have in mind, as in the second argument, is a sort of commingling which Forms which are opposite to each other by nature cannot undergo in relation to each other. This, indeed, is borne out by the text of 255 A 12–B 1, where the consequence which proves that neither Change nor Rest can be identical with Identity or Difference is that the Form concerned would be compelled to change to the opposite of its proper nature. What Plato seems to mean at 255 A 10 is not that the Form of Change cannot be at rest, but that it must be absurd to say that any *particular* change can be at rest. As we remarked in the discussion of the second argument, Plato is driven to abuse, or at least to stretch, the subject–predicate structure in order to cover something more than would be covered by a simple predicative statement in copular form. As in the second argument, and as also in the argument of 255 D, there is a faint whiff of self-predication in the air; and once again there is the suspicion that the cause of Plato's (and his readers') difficulty is his inability to distinguish between the concept which is the expression of the notion of change and the Form which is the nominee of 'Change', and is itself an unchanging thing. Thus the sense of μετέχειν at 255 B 1 must be a stronger sense of participation than corresponds precisely to the copula as used in ordinary language, and the statement κίνησις στήσεται at 255 A 10 must mean something other than 'The Form of Change will be in some sense stable'. Whether what Plato has in mind is a blending amounting more to identity or more to total predication it seems impossible to say. But the argument can now best be expanded somewhat as follows: We must dispose of the possibility that either Change or Rest can be identical with either Identity or Difference. Let us suppose, therefore, that Difference and Change are identical. Now we know that Difference applies to Rest. Therefore Change will apply to Rest. But Rest must also apply to Rest, and Rest is the opposite of Change. Therefore Change cannot apply to Rest as Rest applies to Rest. Therefore Difference cannot apply to Rest as Rest applies to Rest. But we know that Difference can apply to Rest. Therefore Difference cannot be identical with Change.

This is not, perhaps, very satisfactory as an interpretation of an argument both dubious and elliptical. But it is difficult to see how we are to find a way to a readier and simpler interpretation without abandoning the view, based on strong and solid evidence, that Plato believed that it is not false to assert that there is a valid sense in which Rest can be predicated of Change. Unless this view is abandoned, the four arguments in which the relations of Change and Rest are discussed must tell against the view that Plato distinguished by a conscious and deliberate use of μετέχειν the copulative use of εἶναι as such. This conclusion, it has been argued, must be supported also by the use of μετέχειν at 255 D 4, although this argument is likewise difficult to interpret and hardly less elliptically expressed. The result, then, is that although damaging arguments can be brought against Cornford's interpretation of the relevant passages, no satisfactory warrant can be found for attributing to Plato more than a partial discovery of the copula. A final argument for this conclusion is afforded by the fact that Plato in his analysis of negation undertakes no analysis of the difference between negative statements of identity and negative statements of predication. This assertion, however, must involve at least a brief examination of how Plato does in fact conduct his analysis of negation; and it is to this problem that we must now turn.

NEGATION AND DIFFERENCE

The basis of Plato's analysis may be summarized without argument. He has shown himself unable to cope with statements of non-existence; but by elucidating the nature and properties of the Form of Difference he shows that negative statements need not bear non-existential import and that the dictum of Parmenides may accordingly be circumvented. This much at least may stand unquestioned; and although Plato may seem to be unduly troubled by a simple or even an unreal problem— for, after all, he knew quite well that denials can be both made and accepted as meaningful—nevertheless *Sophist* 257B–259B is an ingenious move made in the face of a genuine philosophical problem. For of course Plato knew that denial is possible, just as the late learners knew that you can say 'man is good' or Zeno knew that Achilles could in fact overtake the tortoise.[1] But the philosopher's problem is not solved by conducting meaningful conversation in which negation occurs any more than by running a series of victorious foot-races against tortoises. Plato was in the position of any philosopher faced with a paradox whose solution escapes him. His worry is not to be appeased by demonstrations of fact, but only by refutation of the argument which appears to render the fact impossible. Plato, in the *Sophist*, succeeds, by his analysis of negation and his application of the same analysis to falsehood, in appeasing a worry which had been made both real and explicit on the great authority of Parmenides,[2] and which there is no evidence that Plato himself or any of his predecessors had hitherto been able adequately to appease. Two questions, however, arise out of his analysis of negation to which it will be convenient to attempt an answer before passing on to consider the analysis of falsehood to which the analysis of negation gives rise. The first question is how closely Plato attaches the negative prefix to that from which a difference is being asserted by it. The second, which has already been mentioned, is how far (if at all) he distinguished negative predication from negative identity. These two questions will in turn raise the question of Plato's attitude to the connecting functions

---

[1] Arist. *Phys.* 239b14 ff.

[2] For Plato's own reverence for the authority of Parmenides, cf. (apart from the dialogue which bears his name, and in which some commentators have mistakenly supposed Plato to be parodying him) *Theaet.* 183E, *Soph.* 217C.

of his 'vowel' Forms; and this third question will require separate comment before proceeding to the discussion of falsehood, meaning and the συμπλοκή of Forms.

It is at once clear that Plato is still a long way from an analysis in which the negation is set altogether outside the proposition concerned. His conception of negation was not such as could yield the analysis presupposed by the symbolism of ~ (p), and there is in any case no phrase whereby 'it is not the case that. . .' could be expressed in Greek unless by οὐκ ἔσθ' ὅπως, which implies either impossibility or else mere emphasis of a denial. In fact, Plato makes it explicit at 257B 10–C3 that on his analysis a negative prefix, whether μή or οὐ, signifies only something different from whatever things are denoted by the words which follow it. The language which he subsequently uses even seems to suggest that he might be attempting to analyse, for instance, 'it is not the case that Socrates is just' into 'Socrates partakes of the Form of Difference from justice'. This is suggested both by the assertions that the not-large and the not-beautiful and the not-just are as existent (real) as the Large and the Beautiful and the Just, and also by the analogy drawn between the extensions (257C11 μέρος, D4 μόρια) of Knowledge and Difference. The question, therefore, is less whether Plato comes anywhere near such an analysis of negation as is adopted by contemporary logicians than whether his circumvention of the dictum of Parmenides is in fact an analysis of negation at all. For if he proposes merely to rewrite 'X is not A' into 'X partakes of (not-A)' then he is not explaining negation, but only stretching the scope of assertion in order to cover it. However, there are grounds for arguing that in fact we need not be driven to this conclusion.

In the first place, the analogy between Difference and Knowledge need not be taken to imply this. For Difference, unlike Knowledge, is one of the μέγιστα γένη and as such it has the totality of existents for its extension.[1] The point of the analogy is that as the different exten-

---

[1] See p. 93, n. 1. It is never made clear to how many Forms Plato attributed the quality of total pervasiveness for, as we have seen, he seems to attribute it to Unity although Unity is nowhere described as a μέγιστον γένος and it is not impossible that he might have thought that there were others of which it could also be true. At any rate, it seems safe to say that Plato thought it true of everything to say not simply that it is, but that it is in some sense single, the same (if only as itself), different (from everything else), at rest (if only since denotable) and in change (if only since known). On the question of self-identity, it is interesting to compare paras. 215–16 of Wittgenstein's *Philosophical Investigations*.

sions of Knowledge differ by being Knowledge *of* different things and therefore designated as such, so the different extensions of Difference differ by being different *from* different things and therefore designated as such. But it is still difficult to see just what Plato means by τὸ μὴ καλόν or τὸ μὴ μέγα when spoken of as such. The point which he seems to be making is that Difference is a Form and therefore Difference in relation to Largeness or Beauty is as ontologically reputable as Largeness or Beauty themselves; and it is only Difference as such which is explicitly stated to be a Form (258C3). But he seems also to speak of τὸ μὴ καλόν as though he meant more by the phrase than 'any instance of Difference from Beauty' (257D7–E10). Thus at 257E9–10 he can hardly mean that anything that is not Beauty is as real or existent as Beauty unless he will also maintain that nothing is less real or existent than Beauty; for everything except Beauty itself, however unreal it may be, is different from Beauty. Similarly, the language of 258A7–9 would seem to suggest that the parts (μόρια) of Difference are its sub-species rather than any of its extensions.

The answer to this difficulty seems to lie in the answer to the second of our two initial questions. It cannot be denied that Plato fails to make his meaning entirely clear; and in fact it is quickly demonstrable that he makes no distinction between negative identity and negative predication. He gives no evidence of thinking that his analysis does not satisfy all statements of the form '*X* is not so-and-so'. But he gives no hint of an awareness of the difference between '*X* is not just' and '*X* is not Justice'. Therefore we must analyse both these statements as '*X* partakes of Difference in relation to Justice'. Thus when Plato asserts that τὸ μὴ μέγα and τὸ μὴ καλόν truly are and have their proper nature, he is at once back in the logical morass which is the breeding-ground of self-predication (258B8–C4). It is never clear whether τὸ μὴ καλόν, for instance, means for Plato 'Difference in relation to Beauty' or 'what is different in relation to Beauty' or 'Difference-in-relation-to-Beauty which is a real thing both identitatively and predicatively different from Beauty'. In fact, of course, it is quite true that difference from beauty is different from beauty; but this does not mean that it is not beautiful. Plato, however, in the argument of 258B8–C4, seems to be arguing that non-Being (i.e. Difference) genuinely is not (i.e. is different), just as τὸ μέγα is large and τὸ μὴ μέγα is not large (i.e. partakes of Difference in relation to Largeness). There are only two pos-

sible moves we can make if we wish to acquit Plato of a charge of illegitimate self-predication; either we must take τὸ μέγα at 258 B 10 not to refer to the Form, or we must take all the statements of B 10–C 3 as statements of self-identity. But that it is the Form of τὸ μέγα which is referred to seems clear both from the fact that it is cited to parallel τὸ μὴ ὄν and from 258 A 1 where it is asserted that Difference from Largeness has being just as Largeness (τὸ μέγα αὐτό) does. If, on the other hand, we take Plato to be asserting the self-identity of Largeness, it is hard to see why he should wish to do so or why he should do so in this form. He wishes to say that it is legitimate to assert that τὸ μὴ ὄν (which he has shown can be translated into τὸ μὴ ὄν X, i.e. difference) has its own proper nature (ἐστὶ τὴν αὐτοῦ φύσιν ἔχον),[1] that is to say is itself genuinely not (i.e. different). He does not wish to say that Difference is the same as Difference (i.e. μετέχει ταὐτοῦ πρὸς αὐτό); and if he wished to say that Largeness is Largeness it would be natural to expect τὸ μέγα ἦν τὸ μέγα rather than τὸ μέγα ἦν μέγα which is at the least somewhat misleading. Thus there must remain a strong suspicion that Plato in his analysis of negation not only does not distinguish between being different from large and being different from Largeness, but has even lapsed into his old mistake[2] of thinking that Largeness is something large. If this is really so, it is not surprising that he fails to make clear the distinction between Difference and what is different.

This difficulty, indeed, appears at the beginning of the discussion in the passage (257 B 3–C 3) in which Plato makes the point that if we analyse negation as difference we need not understand denial as entailing the direct contrary of what is denied. He evidently has in mind the principal achievement of his analysis, namely that it shows how

[1] Cf. 255 E where it is said that everything is different by partaking in Difference, not διὰ τὴν αὐτοῦ φύσιν. This, clearly, must be a question of predication and not identity.

[2] The evidence for self-predication has been too much discussed in recent literature to need recapitulation here. If, however, Soph. 258 B–C is in fact an example, it is, as already remarked, the only one which occurs after the Parmenides. Some critics have felt that Plato himself brings such effective arguments against it in the Parmenides that he must have been consciously led to abandon it. However, as I have argued elsewhere, he never does expound any explicit modification of the Theory of Forms such as the serious and valid arguments of the first part of the Parmenides would appear to require, nor, although he expresses his continuing conviction of the theory, does he offer any adequate solution to the problem of participation. It is not, therefore, by any means inconceivable that he should still lapse into the language of self-predication either by inadvertence or because convinced that the difficulties to which it gives rise cannot in fact be as damaging as they appear.

negation need not involve an assertion of non-existence. But the example, or analogy, that he gives is that in saying that something is not large we may mean that it is equal just as well as that it is small. It must be predication that is in question here, for to say that something is not identical with τὸ μέγα does not make it identical with either τὸ ἴσον or τὸ σμικρόν any more than with τὸ δίκαιον or τὸ καλόν. But the natural assumption that ὅταν εἴπωμέν τι μὴ μέγα must mean 'whenever we say that something is (copula) not big' is less secure if we allow ourselves to be reminded of *Phaedo* 74A9–10 where φαμέν πού τι εἶναι ἴσον is without question a reference to the Form of Equal itself. Plato could, in fact, be saying that when we assert the existence of Difference from Largeness, we are not necessarily talking about Smallness rather than Equality. It is also possible that, as Cornford[1] believes, the whole discussion is still within the world of Forms. This is perhaps not very likely, since particulars as much as Forms must also be μόρια of Difference, and Plato's analysis of negation will not be very satisfactory if it only covers the world of Forms. But since it is unfortunately the case that Plato does not make himself clear, it is only possible to conclude that he was not fully aware of the importance of distinguishing both between denial of predication and denial of identity and between Forms and their extensions.

Plato's language in this passage, therefore, need not compel us to the conclusion that he proposed merely to set up Forms of not-Beautiful, not-Just etc. to fit every separate case where a denial is made. His language is indeed sufficiently ambiguous to be not incompatible with such an analysis, if there were any other evidence in favour of it. But such an analysis is not necessarily entailed by the language; and in fact there is considerable evidence against it. There is not only the evidence of the *Politicus* that Plato denied the rank of Forms to not-Greek and not-ten-thousand, but also the evidence of Alexander that the Academy did not recognize such Forms as not-wood and not-white.[2] Moreover, apart from the fact that setting up separate negative Forms would not contribute an explanation of denial at all, Plato does not explicitly ascribe the status of Form to anything other than Difference itself (258c3). Although it is unclear when exactly he is talking about particulars and when about Forms, it is clear that he believes both that what is not beautiful is as legitimately existent as what is beautiful and

---

[1] Cornford, pp. 290, 293–4; cf. p. 291, n. 2.   [2] See p. 60, n. 1.

that Difference in relation to Beauty is as ontologically respectable as Beauty itself. Moreover, any Form will be different from Beauty without thereby becoming any less real; and although Plato presumably did not believe that everything that is not Beauty is as real as Beauty, he presumably did believe that it is possible to assert of anything that it is not Beauty without implying thereby any diminution of its existential status, whatever that might be.[1] Plato could hold all these propositions to be true without positing negative Forms; and indeed it would appear despite the imprecision of his language that he in fact did so. This cannot be said to constitute a complete and satisfactory analysis of the notion of negation; and it affords strong support for our previous conclusion that Plato did not entirely distinguish between the copulative and identitative senses of εἶναι. But it nevertheless affords an adequate circumvention of the dictum of Parmenides, and thereby paves the way for the analysis of false statement which is the stock-in-trade of the elusive Sophist.

CONNECTION BETWEEN FORMS

Before, however, passing on to false statement it is necessary to make some remarks on the role of logical connection which Plato appears to assign to certain Forms. Plato's use of μετέχειν makes it not implausible to suggest[2] that without elevating it to the status of a Form he assigns to it the function of joining one Form to another according to the rules established in the discussion of the μέγιστα γένη. But this view must in fact be ruled out by the passage from 252E to 253C in which the

---

[1] It is, however, possible that Plato did not have in mind such a proposition as 'this table is not identical with the Form of Identity', but only considered possible statements of non-identity between entities of equal ontological standing. Such examples as he gives do not enable the question to be definitely settled one way or the other. At 257A 4–6, where Being is said to not be an unlimited number of things, this could cover non-identity with particulars as well as Forms. But the next sentence (257A8–10) does seem to imply that Plato has only other Forms in mind, as in the case of Change at 256D–E, from which the conclusion is generalized. At 256E 5–6, where it can only be predication that is meant since no Form can be identical with any other than itself, the conclusion is accordingly in terms of Forms only, since to say, for example, that Identity is single is to assert no more than a relation between two Forms (ταὐτὸν μετέχει τοῦ ἑνός). Thus although 257A4–6 must almost certainly be an assertion of non-identity (unless Plato means instead, or also, that Being partakes predicatively of itself but not of Largeness or Circularity), it is at least likely that by τἆλλα Plato has in mind, as Cornford maintains, no more than all other Forms.

[2] This view is in fact advanced by Ackrill (2), p. 1.

analogy is drawn between the vowels in the alphabet and certain Forms. Here quite clearly Plato implies that some Kinds (i.e. Forms)[1] will be shown to pervade all the others[2] in such a way that they are able to blend (συμμείγνυσθαι). Thus presumably Plato uses μετέχειν only to symbolize a relation of connection which is in fact performed by the Forms themselves. But this does not solve all the problems raised by the question of connection. Let us take, for example, the statement 'Identity is not Difference'. This must translate into 'Identity partakes of Difference from (in relation to) Difference'. If we wish to attribute to Plato for a moment a possible formulation of a distinction which we have seen he did not in fact arrive at, we may even translate this into 'Identity partakes of Difference in relation to Identity in relation to Difference', or in other words 'Identity is not the same as Difference'. In this analysis, the connecting function of the vowel-Form of Difference is adequate to cover the relation to Identity with Difference of the entity (namely Identity itself) which is being asserted to be non-identical with Difference; but it cannot cover the relation of partaking which is asserted at the outset of the analysis to subsist between Identity and Difference. μετέχειν itself does not stand for a Form; and if it did, there would at once arise a regress of the most glaringly vicious kind, for we should have to posit a second μέθεξις to connect the first μέθεξις with the Forms which it is supposed to connect with each other. As it is, there is the faint aroma of a regress about any assertion that two Forms are connected by a third. But it is not the Form of Connection to which Plato attributes this function. It must be, in fact, the Form of Being which has the property symbolized by the relation of μέθεξις and which enables it to perform the role of the copula. But what, then, are we to make of such a statement as κίνησις ἔστι διὰ τὸ μετέχειν τοῦ ὄντος? It cannot be the function of Being to connect Change with Being, although in such a statement as κίνησις ἔστηκε διὰ τὸ μετέχειν στάσεως (i.e. κίνησίς ἐστι στάσιμος) it is Being which connects Change with Rest. Perhaps we should follow the suggestion that Plato's assimilation of the existential and copulative senses of Being amounts to the obliteration of the difference. In this case, κίνησις μετέχει τοῦ

---

[1] Cf. Cornford, p. 261, n. 1; Bluck (3), p. 181, n. 5.

[2] διὰ πάντων at 253 C 1 could mean 'everything', not merely all other Forms, for Plato certainly believed that particulars could stand in a relation to the μέγιστα γένη and indeed (see p. 100, n. 1) must do so. But from the context it would appear that he has only Forms in mind.

ὄντος symbolizes the connection of Change to an as yet incomplete Being, just as κίνησις μετέχει τοῦ μὴ ὄντος must mean that Change is not something-or-other (as yet unspecified). But since grounds have been shown for arguing that Plato, although he did not fully distinguish the existential sense of εἶναι as such, nevertheless did not wholly assimilate it to the copulative sense, we must conclude that he meant by κίνησις ἔστι διὰ τὸ μετέχειν τοῦ ὄντος that Being has the property of blending with Change (and indeed everything else) as well as with whatever other Form (including Sameness in relation to itself or something else) there may be to which Change stands in a relation of predication.

We may further support this analysis by carrying the vowel analogy beyond where Plato does himself. For the fact is that a vowel does not need to connect two consonants in order to form a word; but every word must contain at least one vowel. 'Bet' and 'be' are both words, but 'bt' cannot be; or, to take a Greek example, τῶν and ὤν are both words, but τν cannot be. No further letter is needed to connect vowels to consonants or to each other, although the order of the letters is of course significant (thus κίνησις μετέχει τοῦ ὄντος does not mean the same as τὸ ὂν μετέχει κινήσεως). What is perhaps more important, however, is that the Form of Being must occur in every combination where the relation of the terms is that of subject and predicate. This covers not only those statements which are unmistakably of this form, such as κίνησίς ἐστι στάσιμος, but also all statements of the form of noun and verb, such as κίνησις ἔστηκεν. In fact, as we shall see from Plato's own analysis of statement, Being must occur in all statements, since all statements must depend upon a combination of nouns and verbs. This does not mean that all combinations involve Being, for to assert that Change is different from Identity does not require Being to connect Difference and Identity (or Difference in relation to Identity with Identity) but only to connect Change with Difference. But it means that Being occurs in all cases of combination symbolized by μέθεξις and this means that Being occurs in every statement. This is a conclusion which it must be admitted that Plato does not make explicit. But it must follow from the fact that he assigns to the vowel-Forms the function of combination and does not give any evidence that he includes μέθεξις among their number.

This conclusion may help to throw light on the puzzling assertion made at 259E that all λόγος (which may mean statement, or meaning, or discourse, or all three) owes its existence to the interweaving of Forms (διὰ γὰρ τὴν ἀλλήλων τῶν εἰδῶν συμπλοκὴν ὁ λόγος γέγονεν ἡμῖν). This sentence occurs in the passage which constitutes the transition from the discussion of the μέγιστα γένη and the analysis of negation to the analysis of statement, meaning and false statement. The results of the analysis of negation whereby the dictum of Parmenides has been circumvented are first of all summarized in a brief résumé which runs from 258c to 259D.[1] The Stranger then observes that the isolation of everything from everything else[2] involves the total abolition of logos, for logos owes its existence to the interweaving of Forms. Theaetetus expresses puzzlement as to why agreement is required at this point about the nature of logos (260B), but it is pointed out to him by the Stranger that now that non-Being has been explained it remains to show how it can combine with statement to produce the falsity (ψεῦδος) which the Sophist will either deny to be real or will deny to be applicable to statement (260B–261c). The discussion then proceeds to the analysis first of statement and then of false statement (261c ff.).

Just what Plato means by the 'interweaving of Forms' and how he believes that this interweaving makes logos possible it is extremely difficult to establish with any confidence. The question has been the

---

[1] Plato seems, in this summary, to have only non-identity in mind (259A6–B6). However, he asserts at B5–6 that Being *is* in many ways (πολλαχῇ) as well as that it *is not* in many ways. This cannot mean that Being is identical with many other things (cf. 256E5–6 περὶ ἕκαστον ἄρα τῶν εἰδῶν πολὺ μέν ἐστι τὸ ὄν which likewise cannot mean every Form is identical with many other things, although in the subsequent discussion Plato seems only to have non-identity in mind), for such an assertion would be false. It is impossible to say whether Plato consciously meant predication in these two places, but it seems more likely that he was not in fact conscious of the need to make the distinction. At 257B6–7, however, he must, as already pointed out, have negative predication in mind.

[2] 260A1–B2 seems to be a reference back to 252A–C, where it is argued that the admission of the possibility of σύμμειξις will dispose of the protagonists of all the theories previously discussed. This point is then effectively made against the late learners. They assert that no combinations of ὀνόματα are possible; but by so doing they deprive themselves of the claim to validity of the assertion that no combinations of ὀνόματα are possible, for they cannot make their assertion without in fact combining ὀνόματα. Similarly, if they assert that all statements are statements of identity they can only enunciate their claim in the form of a proposition which is not a statement of identity. This move against the late learners' position is a valid and powerful one. But, of course, it is not by itself enough. For the late learners require to be shown not merely that their position is self-stultifying, but also what their mistake was which led them to adopt it, just as the solipsist, although he may allow that he cannot cite any criterion for the validity of his position, still demands evidence adequate to satisfy him that it is incorrect.

subject of much recent discussion,[1] but attention has largely been concentrated on the part played in specifically false statement by the interweaving of Forms. It is necessary, however, to explain also just how the interweaving of Forms shows us that 'walks runs sleeps' or 'lion deer horse' is not a statement, but 'man learns' is. In the remarks which follow no systematic attempt will be made to show why the interpretations put forward by others cannot be regarded as entirely satisfactory. It will, however, be suggested that although Plato himself may not be entirely clear on certain points in his analysis (which means that no definitive interpretation is possible), nevertheless a view may be put forward[2] which appears in some respects, at least, to be an improvement on any hitherto maintained. One important point must be borne in mind from the outset. It is nowhere made clear in the text whether Plato means that the interweaving of Forms must be represented in every statement or merely presupposed by it; and it may be that Plato did not explicitly mean either one of these without the other. With this in mind, we may turn to a closer examination of the text. But before directly considering the problem of συμπλοκή, some more general remarks should be made on Plato's attitude to meaning, statement and truth.

MEANING AND STATEMENT

The section of the argument on meaning and statement runs from 261 c to 262 e. Here it is established that of the two kinds of words which serve to designate something (261 e 5–6 περὶ τὴν οὐσίαν δηλω-μάτων διττὸν γένος), namely nouns and verbs,[3] a succession of one

---

[1] Cornford, pp. 300–17; Ross, pp. 115–16; Hackforth (2); Robinson (2); Peck; Ackrill (1); Hamlyn (1); Bluck (3).

[2] My own view is not very dissimilar to that of Mr J. M. E. Moravcsik, to whom I am indebted for correspondence and discussion on this point.

[3] It may be questioned whether 'noun' and 'verb' are a legitimate translation of ὄνομα and ῥῆμα, since these words imply a clear and technical differentiation from other specific parts of speech. Perhaps better are Dürr's equivalents, Hauptwort and Tätigkeitswort, which he defines respectively (p. 191) as 'ein Wort, welches die Personen, welche die Handlungen ausführen, bezeichnet' and 'ein Wort, welches eine Handlung bezeichnet'. It seems clear from this passage that prepositions or conjunctions did not qualify for Plato as ὀνόματα (cf. Cornford, p. 307, citing Plutarch, Plat. Qu. x) and did not therefore stand for Forms. Adjectives and adverbs, presumably, stand for the same Form as the noun derived from them or from which they derive. Plato appears to have classed all words which are not ὀνόματα in their own right (including pronouns) among the terms which are described in Socrates' 'dream' (Theaet. 202 A) as 'running about and attaching themselves

without the other does not constitute a statement. Every statement, in fact, must contain at least one noun and one verb if it is to mean anything as opposed to merely naming (262D 3–4 οὐκ ὀνομάζει μόνον ἀλλά τι περαίνει). Any such combination, even of the simplest kind, is adequate to constitute a statement (262C). The example in fact given is ἄνθρωπος μανθάνει (262C9), which gives information by weaving together (συμπλέκων) verb and noun (262D). Thus Plato is saying not only that every statement must contain a verb and noun and that every combination of verb and noun produces a statement, but he is also saying that every statement has meaning. Meaning, in fact, does not depend upon what it is that is represented but upon the structure of the representation. Plato does not wish, as some twentieth-century philosophers have done, to legislate over criteria of meaning, except in a very limited sense. He does say that only statements can be meaningful (as opposed to performing only the function of denotation), but he does not say that anything can be a statement and not have meaning. On Plato's analysis, such statements as 'Thursday gargles' or 'justice is an egg' or 'the Agora is dreaming' are perfectly meaningful. They do not happen to be true; but that is another matter altogether.

From this he goes on to say that every statement must be about something,[1] and must possess the character of being either true or false (262E–263B). It is clear that he never considered statements whose subject is 'the present king of France' or 'the round square cupola on top of Berkeley College'. But what is more surprising is his apparent belief that every combination of noun and verb must be a statement and as such must be either true or false. Aristotle is well aware that this is not the case (de Interpr. 16b33–17a7), for he observes that whereas every λόγος is σημαντικός not every one is ἀποφαντικός, that is to say, either true or false. Thus prayer, for instance, is λόγος, but it is neither true nor false; but Aristotle's concern is with ἀποφαντικὸς λόγος only, and he dismisses the rest as an enquiry more related to the study of oratory or poetry. Now it is not surprising that we should not find in the *Sophist* the distinction between σημαντικός and ἀποφαντικὸς λόγος (of which latter, indeed, Aristotle goes on to give an analysis[2] not very

to everything', but he never conducts anything amounting to a systematic classification of parts of speech. Once these preliminary remarks have been made, however, 'noun' and 'verb' are probably the best English equivalents for ὄνομα and ῥῆμα.

[1] For the simple genitive used at 262E5–6, see Cornford, p. 308, n. 1.

[2] *De Interpr.* 17a9–10 ἀνάγκη δὲ πάντα λόγον ἀποφαντικὸν ἐκ ῥήματος εἶναι ἢ πτώσεως.

dissimilar to Plato's analysis of statement). Nor is it surprising that Plato does not attempt to set up criteria by which he could avoid what we might call in a more sophisticated terminology category mistakes.[1] What is surprising is that he is not prepared to admit as λόγος anything but a true-or-false subject–predicate statement.

This surprise is increased if we recall the passage of the *Protagoras* (347E) where Plato speaks of poets as περὶ πράγματος διαλεγόμενοι ὃ ἀδυνατοῦσι ἐξελέγξαι,[2] for he here seems to imply that the utterances of poets, though not without meaning, are nevertheless not susceptible of verification. He was not, of course, concerned at the time of writing the *Protagoras* to attempt an analysis of statement. But he surely thought that some utterances are meaningful which are not of the form 'man learns' and are not either true or false.[3] Indeed, it is tempting to say merely that Plato in the *Sophist* does not happen to have in mind imprecation or exhortation or poetry or prayer. But the fact is that he makes no provision for these in his analysis, as Aristotle does in his. It may be that he would allow them also to have meaning (περαίνειν τι or δηλοῦν τι) although they cannot be true or false, and it may be that he is here consciously using λόγος in a restricted sense of statement of a verifiable kind only. But he does not say so; and we are left with an analysis in which meaning is equated with statement as here defined. Thus Plato has now shown how combination of Forms (and so of ὀνόματα) is possible, how negation can be so analysed as to circumvent the dictum of Parmenides, and how meaning is constituted by statement. Of none of these can he be regarded as giving a complete analysis; but each one marks an interesting and important step forward in the face of problems previously unsolved. Having established how we can say truly and meaningfully that X is or is not A, it only remains to establish how we can meaningfully but falsely assert one of these same propositions.

---

[1] E.g. such mistakes as are involved in supposing that the Agora can be said to be dreaming or not dreaming, Thursday gargling or not gargling, and justice either just or unjust (as at *Prot.* 330C).

[2] Cf. *Gorg.* 508A–B ἢ ἐξελεγκτέος δὴ οὗτος ὁ λόγος ἡμῖν ἐστιν...ἢ εἰ οὗτος ἀληθής ἐστιν, σκεπτέον τί τὰ συμβαίνοντα.

[3] It is necessary to notice that Plato nowhere says that *only* statement can be true or false (this will become important later). He only says that statement *must* be true or false and that nouns or verbs combined only with their own kind do not constitute statement. This does not mean either that individual words do not have meaning in the sense that they perform a legitimate function of denotation, or that truth and falsehood can reside only in statement.

Συμπλοκὴ εἰδῶν

Before, however, considering Plato's analysis of false statement, there remains to be settled the question of how meaningful statement (i.e. statement) represents or presupposes an interweaving of Forms. The most recent commentator upon this problem[1] understands Plato to mean that in any statement we make we are in fact weaving Forms together, whether correctly or incorrectly; and when we say, for instance, that 'Theaetetus is sitting' we are weaving together the Form Man and the Form Sitting. Now it is possible that this is in fact what Plato thought. But before accepting this interpretation, we must first ask just what the relation is which we assert between Man and Sitting when we say that Theaetetus sits. It is obviously not that of species and genus or that of identity. But it can hardly be that of predication, either, for this would mean that the Form of Man is in fact seated somewhere. Perhaps we should at this point be right simply to convict Plato of his old confusion between Largeness and a supremely Large thing or, in this case, between Manhood and a sort of supremely manly super-Man. The language of 262D could certainly be read to suggest that when we weave together a noun and a verb we weave together the Form for which the noun stands and the Form for which the verb stands. On this analysis, the problem is solved simply by being removed to a higher level. 'Man learns' is a statement because a man can be said to learn, whereas 'walks runs' is not a statement because 'walks' cannot be said to run; in other words, the Form Man can do a sort of super-Learning, but the Form Walking, being the Form of a verb, cannot indulge in any super-Running or indeed any other activity, even if a super-Activity. This, obviously, is not very satisfactory as an analysis. But if we are to believe that 'Man learns' is a statement because the Form Man blends with the Form Learning, then it can only be something like this that Plato means.

It cannot be ruled out that this is what Plato does mean. But if we remember his remarks upon the function of the vowel-Forms, it becomes clear that an alternative interpretation is possible. In the first place, it is in fact the case that what makes a statement is not the assertion of a relation between Forms (although, of course, Forms can be and often are the subjects of statements) but the assertion of a

[1] Bluck (3), p. 182.

relation between any particular (such as Theaetetus) and a Form (such as Sitting). To say that Theaetetus sits is not to make a statement about the Form of Man any more than about Beauty or Snub-nosedness, although Theaetetus is beautiful and snub-nosed as well as being a man. Plato himself makes it quite clear that the statement 'Theaetetus sits' or 'Theaetetus flies' is about nothing and no one other than the Theaetetus to whom the Stranger is talking (263 A). What we do when we say that Theaetetus sits is to assert a relation of μέθεξις between Theaetetus and Sitting; that is to say, Theaetetus partakes of Being in relation to Sitting. It is because Being has the property of blending (or connecting) with Sitting, and Theaetetus is (like everything else that there is) one of the extensions of Being, that we can legitimately assert (whether truly or falsely) that Theaetetus sits. On this interpretation, we may, if we wish, say that interweaving of Forms is represented by every statement, since every statement involves the interweaving of Being and the Form for which the predicate of the sentence stands. But perhaps we need only understand Plato to be saying (259 E) that the capacity of Forms to interweave with each other (as demonstrated in the preceding argument) is what makes logos (that is, meaningful statement) possible.

What, then, are we to make of 'walks runs sleeps' or 'lion deer horse'? Here, the answer is simply not that these successions of words represent an impossible blending of Forms, but that they do not assert any blending at all. As we have seen, meaning depends for Plato on structure, not content.[1] It is perfectly possible to assert a relation between, for instance, the Form Lion and the Form Horse, or between an individual lion and the Form of Horse, or between an individual lion and an individual horse; but the form of words 'lion horse' does not do so. All such statements would involve the interweaving of Forms, even the last; for to say as little as, for instance, 'this lion is that horse' is still to say 'this lion partakes of Being in relation to Identity in relation to that horse'. But to say 'lion horse' is not to assert any

---

[1] Plato does not consider such forms of words as whatever would be a Greek equivalent of 'slithy toves gyre and gimble'. We may conjecture that he would say that this sentence is meaningless simply because the words of which it is composed are meaningless, not because it is not a sentence. But this might then involve him in saying that 'toves' must be a member of the anomalous class of non-existents. This problem clearly did not occur to him, so that it is perhaps pointless to speculate as to his reactions to it.

sort of relation.[1] Thus Plato's analysis of meaning and statement is entirely compatible with his assertion that all meaningful statement not only presupposes the possibility of the interweaving of Forms, but even represents such an interweaving. Moreover this interweaving need not be between any Form (except Being itself) of which the subject of the statement is an extension and the Form represented by the predicate word. Plato may have believed this to be the case; but if so, he is guilty of a confusion which we are not required to attribute to him.

THE DISCUSSION OF FALSE STATEMENT

From this point we may now turn to the passage in which Plato shows how a meaningful statement can nevertheless be false (262 D–263 E). In the *Theaetetus*, at the beginning of the discussion of error, Socrates had remarked in passing that it must be a contradiction in terms to say that it is possible for anyone to think truly what is false (189 C–D). This paradox Plato now vindicates by showing that a statement which is really and truly false is in fact possible (263 D 4 ὄντως τε καὶ ἀληθῶς γίγνεσθαι λόγος ψευδής). The passage in which Plato's actual analysis is given is brief and concise, and this fact has of itself caused concern to commentators. However, it should be remembered that the analysis of negation, which is the crux of the problem of false statement, has already been given at some length. Furthermore it has already been established that any combination of noun and verb constitutes a statement. All that remains, therefore, is to show by means of an example of a simple and obviously false statement how there is a legitimate connection between the two.

The example which Plato gives, in contrast to the true statement 'Theaetetus is sitting (κάθηται)', is 'Theaetetus, to whom I am now speaking, is flying (πέτεται)'. This emphasis on the fact that it is the Theaetetus to whom the Stranger is speaking who is the subject of the false statement is presumably made in order to avoid the move whereby

---

[1] The only difficult case is such a sentence as ὅδε ὁ ἵππος ἔστιν. Plato does not anywhere discuss such a case, and it may never have occurred to him. But it may perhaps be cited as a further argument against his having distinguished the existential sense of εἶναι. Such a use of εἶναι he might have argued to be incomplete (just as ὅδε ὁ ἵππος οὐκ ἔστι [ἔστι μὴ ὄν] would be) and therefore not yet to assert a relation between Forms. 'This horse is the same as itself', on the other hand, would be a complete use. But again, any opinion as to his view must be almost wholly speculative.

according to the atomistic position of the *Cratylus* the statement could be pronounced true of some other Theaetetus. Plato has now explicitly emancipated himself from the assimilation of stating and naming; and his present analysis rules out the view on which all mistakes are likened to that of saying 'Hello, Hermogenes' to Cratylus. His choice, however, of an obviously false statement is an unfortunate one for two reasons. In the first place, it may be one which he believed to be not merely observably false, but necessarily impossible; and in the second, it may be one which he selected because it is incompatible with the example given of a true statement about the same Theaetetus to whom the Stranger is at the moment speaking. It is obviously impossible to assert categorically that Plato did not select his example for either or both of these reasons. But it is equally obviously the case that there is a limitless number of false statements which can be made which do not fall under either of these headings. It may be that Plato has incompatibility in mind. But this is an interpretation which is itself not immune from objection,[1] and it is surely worth trying to see whether there is not a feasible interpretation whereby Plato's analysis covers all false statements. It is perfectly plausible to suggest that Plato selected his example for no further ulterior purpose than to give a proposition which nobody could conceivably maintain to be true. It is, perhaps, too obviously false an example, for the reasons given above. But there is no initial reason why we should suppose that Plato does not believe his analysis to cover any and all cases of falsehood. He may only be setting out to demonstrate that at least some truly false statements are possible; but he appears to be satisfied that he is doing more than this, since he never describes his aim as merely to vindicate the validity of one kind of false statement, and could hardly feel he had really overcome the Sophist's second line of defence (260D–E) if the Sophist could still maintain a whole series of false propositions while denying the possibility of their falsity.

We may therefore consider how Plato's analysis may apply also to

---

[1] I do not, as already stated, propose to argue these objections here. But some valid criticism of the incompatibility view may be found in Bluck (3), although I have already dissented from the view of the interweaving of Forms which is there maintained. Cornford's analysis (pp. 312–17) must be unsatisfactory if only because Cornford keeps the problem as misnaming, on the model of the *Theaetetus*, with the sole (and, as we have seen, erroneous) difference that the *Sophist* introduces the Forms, which the *Theaetetus* did not.

such statements as are neither necessarily false nor incompatible with some other known true fact about Theaetetus. It will perhaps be convenient to begin by offering a translation of 263 B 4–D 4:

STR. Of these statements, the true one states as they are the things
5   that are the case about you.
TH. Of course.
STR. But the false one states things different from the things that are the case.
TH. Yes.
STR. So it states things that are not as things that are.
10 TH. I suppose so.
STR. But the things that it states are things that are, although different from the things that are the case about you.[1] For we said that about everything there are many things that are the case and many that are not.[2]
TH. Yes indeed.
C   STR. The second statement which I made about you must in the first place, according to our definition of what statement is, be itself necessarily one of the shortest possible.
TH. That is what we agreed just now.
5   STR. But it must also be about something or someone.
TH. Just so.
STR. And if it is not about you, it is not about anything or anyone else.
TH. Certainly.
STR. But if it were not about anything or anyone, it would not
10 even be a statement at all; for we showed that it was impossible that there should be a statement which was not a statement about anyone or anything.
TH. Quite right.
D   STR. So when things are said about you such that things that are different are said to be the same and things that are not the case to be things that are, a combination of this kind, which is made up of nouns and verbs, does definitely appear really and truly to constitute false statement.

The use of the phrase 'to be the case' may seem to require some defence or explanation, but the grounds for adopting it will become clear from the interpretation to be given. What is clear from the start

---

[1] Taking ὄντων here as do Burnet and Cornford. ὄντων *Cornarius:* ὄντως *BT.*
[2] The reference is presumably to 256E (περὶ ἕκαστον ἄρα τῶν εἰδῶν πολὺ μέν ἐστι τὸ ὄν, ἄπειρον δὲ πλήθει τὸ μὴ ὄν).

is the emphasis placed on the fact that both examples are statements about Theaetetus; and it is also clear that the analysis depends on the identification of non-Being and Difference. As far as the interweaving of Forms is concerned, its relevance is in fact more readily discernible than in the case of a true statement, for Difference (which must somehow interweave with the predicate Form in a false statement) is more clearly emphasized in the analysis of false statement than Being in the analysis of statement as such. In both cases, we may say that the capacity of certain Forms to make interweaving possible, as described and exemplified in the discussion of the μέγιστα γένη, is the necessary presupposition which makes the λόγος possible. The difference is that a false statement, although it asserts an interweaving, as it must do in order to be a statement at all, does not assert the interweaving on which its actual falsity depends. It does not, in fact, assert the non-identity of the predicate Form with the Forms of those predicates which are in fact the case about (i.e. applicable to) Theaetetus; but it is this non-identity (i.e. interweaving with Difference) which is what accounts for the falsity of any and all false statements.

It can hardly be disputed that flying is different from sitting, nor that if Theaetetus is sitting then he cannot be flying. But Flying is also different from a great number of Forms of which Theaetetus may partake by way of the Form of Being but which do not at all rule out the possible truth of the assertion that Theaetetus is flying. Let us take, for example, the statement 'Theaetetus is a shoemaker', and let us also suppose that this statement is in fact false. Now the Form of Shoemaking is of course different from the Form of Flying or the Form of Sitting or indeed any other Form whatever.[1] But it may quite well be that none of the Forms which can be truly predicated of Theaetetus is incompatible with his being a shoemaker. He may be a tall, snub-nosed, beautiful, seated geometer. But even if he is a geometer by profession, this does not categorically rule out the possibility that he makes an occasional pair of shoes. There may be one or more true

---

[1] The fact of synonyms may seem to call for some qualification of this assertion. But Plato's answer to synonyms is that they are presumably two names for the same Form. Thus when he identifies non-Being with Difference he means simply that when we say that something partakes of non-Being we can only mean that it partakes of Difference (in relation to something as yet unspecified). Similarly, Plato nowhere attempts to deny meaning to foreign languages, although they may require translation to make the communication of meaning possible (cf. *Charm.* 159A, *Meno* 82B, cited in p. 31, n. 1; also *Theaet.* 163B).

predicates of Theaetetus which make it impossible that he should be a shoemaker; for he might have lost both hands in battle, or it might (for Plato) be the case that the known fact of his being a gentleman would be incompatible with his being a shoemaker. But it is quite possible that no such consideration should apply, and that we should nevertheless be able to assert falsely that Theaetetus is a shoemaker. In this case, we are driven to say that Shoemaking is non-identical with any of the Forms to which it is in fact the case that Theaetetus stands in a relation of predication.

This suggests a somewhat cumbrous analysis, for it envisages a procedure somewhat as follows: Let us suppose we wish to vindicate the falsity of the statement 'Theaetetus is a shoemaker'. We must then presumably establish an exhaustive list of all the true predicates of Theaetetus. For each of these a proof of non-identity with Shoemaking must then be established. Thus, Theaetetus is a man; but Manhood is not Shoemaking, because in our language not all men are shoemakers by definition; Theaetetus also is a geometer; but Geometry is not Shoemaking, etc. By this means, the falsity of the statement 'Theaetetus is a shoemaker' will be validly established. This, of course, will be a very laborious undertaking indeed. But in fact Plato's analysis does not in the least preclude the legitimacy of short-cutting the procedure. To illustrate this point, it will be better to revert to his own example of 'Theaetetus flies', since 'Theaetetus is a shoemaker' is not immediately obvious as a falsehood, and raises awkward problems of verification (we might, for instance, feel the need to put Theaetetus down in a shoemaker's workshop and see what sort of a performance he could put up). But the non-identity of Flying with any other Form can surely be assumed without separate proof; and that Flying is not one of the Forms which is here and now applicable to Theaetetus can be settled by simple observation. We see that Theaetetus is not flying as soon as we look at Theaetetus, and we already know that since non-Being is to be equated with Difference no statement need be held to involve non-existential import. Thus when we assert that Theaetetus is flying we neither assert that Theaetetus stands in a relation to something non-existent (this is the point of 263 B 11), nor do we name by the phrase 'Theaetetus-flying' a non-existent item in the furniture of the world, nor are we saying anything about the other Forms of which Theaetetus partakes. But we know that Flying is a Form, and that as such it is different from any and all other Forms. Therefore we can legitimately assert a relation between Theaetetus and Flying although (or, in a sense, because) Flying is different from any of the Forms of which it is true that Theaetetus partakes.

It is tempting to go on from this to say that Plato is arguing that a false statement is a meaningful statement which asserts something other than the facts. But the use of the word fact is likely to be misleading, for Plato says only that a false statement asserts a relation between the subject and a different Form from any Form to which the subject does stand in such a relation. Plato is not here concerned either with how we may verify a statement of whose truth or falsehood we are in doubt or how we may come to believe a statement that is false. His aim is only to controvert the Sophist's position according to which thought and speech cannot have the share of non-Being which they must have if falsehood is to be possible. This he does by showing that since difference is possible, what we do when we enunciate a false statement is to assert that its subject partakes of a Form which is not (i.e. is different from) any of the Forms of which it does partake. It is in this sense, and this sense only, that it says what is not as though it were (263 B 9). Plato's analysis is not such as could be made to yield some formalization like $\sim [(\exists x) (x$ is Theaetetus. Theaetetus is flying$)]$, for we have seen that Plato's notion of Difference, on which the analysis of falsehood depends, does not involve a notion of negation whereby the symbol of negation can be put outside the proposition to be denied. On the other hand, his analysis does show that in the formula 'X is (i.e. partakes of Being in relation to) F', any Form may be read as a value of F for the statement to be meaningful, and the blending properties of Difference make it possible for such a Form not to be any of those to which X does stand in a relation of Being with the result that the statement is meaningful but false.

The interpretation of Plato's analysis of false statement as dependent upon the non-identity of the predicate Form with those Forms to which the subject in fact stands in a relation of predication cannot be claimed as altogether a new one. But such an interpretation requires to be combined with a reasonable interpretation of what Plato says about the interweaving of Forms and the structure of statement in general. Further, it requires to be argued somewhat more fully than has hitherto been done how this analysis may cover all false statements, not merely (as some commentators would have us believe) those dependent upon a necessary incompatibility. There remains to be considered only one category of false statement which may not be immediately apparent as covered by Plato's analysis in the *Sophist*, namely the old mis-naming mistake of the *Cratylus* which could be put into the form of the false statement 'Hermogenes is Cratylus'. This, clearly, is a different sort of false statement from 'Theaetetus is flying'. Here, Hermogenes is being linked by Being to Identity with Cratylus. Identity we may properly regard as the predicate Form necessary to make the statement a statement. But of course it will not do to say that 'Hermogenes is Cratylus' is truly false because Identity is different from Cratylus. We are required to say (analogously with our analysis of Difference) that Identity in relation to Cratylus is non-identical with Identity in relation to Hermogenes (of which it is of course true that Hermogenes partakes). Once we see (following the argument of *Soph.* 256A10–B4) that 'Hermogenes is Cratylus' means 'Hermogenes partakes of Identity with Cratylus' we see how such a false statement can in fact fit into Plato's analysis. That the analysis is still an imperfect one is clear from the preceding discussion. But it satisfactorily overwhelms the Sophist's second line of defence by demonstrating that non-Being (as expounded in terms of Difference) can properly blend with statement and therefore make false statement possible.

From this, Plato goes on to say (263D–264B) that false judgement is also covered by this analysis since a judgement is no more than an unspoken statement, although the judgement may arise as the result of perception. No further description is given of the actual process by which a false judgement comes to be made, but, as was pointed out in the discussion of the treatment of error in the *Theaetetus*, this analysis is applied in the *Philebus* to a specific example of false judgement.[1] There it becomes clear how Plato's analysis of false statement and assimilation to false statement of false judgement enables him to describe false judgement in terms of a model superior to the atomistic model of the *Theaetetus*, on which to make a false judgement was to take hold of the wrong piece of knowledge stored in the mind. In the *Philebus*, to make a false judgement is not to mis-name but to mis-state; that is to say, it is to formulate in one's mind a sentence which describes what one believes to be the case but which assigns to its subject a predicate which

[1] *Phil.* 38 c ff., discussed above, pp. 36–7.

is not in fact identical with any of those to which the subject does stand in this relation. Within the terms of this analysis, then, Plato shows in the *Philebus* how a false judgement is a sentence uttered to oneself expressing a proposition which does not correspond to the facts. This correspondence with the facts depends upon the identity of the predicate attributed to the subject of the judgement (for a judgement, being a sentence, must be about someone or something) with one of its actual predicates. It would, indeed, be possible to take 'Theaetetus is flying' as a possible example of false judgement, for it might be conceivable that through some trick or error of vision someone might mistakenly suppose Theaetetus to be flying. But in the *Sophist* Plato is not concerned with how someone might come to believe the palpably false assertion that Theaetetus is flying. He is only concerned to show that statements (and therefore judgements) can be truly false and that the Sophist can therefore be validly described as a user and maker of falsehoods.

Once this conclusion has been established, the definition of the Sophist which was broken off at 236C–D can be resumed. This resumed definition occupies the rest of the dialogue from 264B9 to its conclusion at 268D5. The final definition[1] of the Sophist is of him as insincere and without knowledge, a maker of the semblances of images of human, not divine, productive art. This conclusion is not relevant to the philosophical issues with which we have been concerned, and indeed some critics have doubted whether it is to be taken altogether seriously, particularly in view of the way in which sophistry is linked to the art of purification in one of the preliminary divisions (231B). This question need not concern us here. But before leaving the *Sophist* it will be necessary to consider the answer to our original question of how far Plato came to evolve a notion of truth-value; and an answer to this must involve some further, though limited, consideration of the *Philebus*.

It will first of all be convenient to re-emphasize three points already made. The first is that Plato nowhere considers how exactly a true statement comes to be true. He is concerned to show both how a statement comes to be a statement and how a false statement comes to be a false statement, but that a statement should be a true statement does not seem to occasion him any concern. It may be that he felt that his remarks on statement and on false statement were adequate to cover

[1] A table schematizing the final division is given by Cornford (p. 324).

the question. But in fact they assume that no analysis is needed rather than stating one; and the starting-point of Plato's discussion is that all statements must be true. It therefore appears that Plato's opponents, whom the central section of the *Sophist* is designed to confute, did not challenge the possibility of truth, but only the possibility of falsehood. Thus Plato's purpose in showing that falsehood is possible is achieved without experiencing the need felt by some subsequent philosophers to expound the nature of truth as such. The second point is that although Plato says that all statements are either true or false and that all judgements are merely unspoken statements, he does not thereby confine truth and falsehood to statement only, nor does he thereby commit himself to any modification of what we have seen to be his earlier position on the nature and objects of knowledge. Although knowledge of the proposition that a true statement expresses cannot be plausibly likened to the sort of intellectual touching which Plato seems to mean by knowledge of Forms in the earlier part of the *Theaetetus*, his analysis of statement in the *Sophist* cannot be taken as evidence that he did not still think of the highest knowledge as the direct apprehension of supremely existent entities. The third point is that although Plato in the *Sophist* comes astonishingly close to certain facts about language, it is not in the terms of an enquiry about language that the argument is conducted. Plato's conception of philosophical activity is of enquiry into the nature, properties and relations of Forms; and what we should explain as the logical structure of language is to Plato the ontological structure of reality, or more particularly of certain pervasive Forms which possess the capacity to perform certain necessary functions. With these caveats in mind we may turn to the *Philebus* in the hope of finding out whether the great advances made by Plato in the *Sophist* did in fact lead to a view that intellectual knowledge is essentially propositional. Much of the *Philebus* affords no help in the answering of this question; but the most illuminating section is that in which Plato discusses the ascription of truth and falsity to pleasures as such. From some of the arguments at the end of the dialogue we have already seen that Plato continued to believe that some kinds of knowledge can be truer than others. But from the central section of the dialogue it is also clear that Plato believed that a closer analogy can be drawn between opinion and pleasure than we should ourselves be disposed to consider legitimate.

THE 'PHILEBUS'

We have already remarked that the example of false judgement given by Plato in the *Philebus* is imbedded in a discussion of true and false pleasures which must serve to modify the ascription to Plato of a notion of truth-value. It is of course the case that in English we do not restrict the use of the word 'true' to propositions ('true love' is perhaps the most obvious example). But Plato's aim in the *Philebus* (36c–40E) seems to be to show that pleasures can be true or false in precisely the way that opinions can be true or false, rather than to show that there is some other useful sense in which pleasures can be meaningfully spoken of as true or false. His analysis of false judgement shows how the difficulties of the *Theaetetus* were overcome by the discoveries of the *Sophist*. But this analysis is only introduced in order to help the linguistically improper analogy between opinion and pleasure.[1]

Throughout the *Philebus*, it is difficult for the modern reader not to feel sympathy with Protarchus rather than with Socrates. At the very beginning of the dialogue (12c–13E), although Socrates is right in arguing that there are different kinds of pleasure just as there are different kinds of colour or shape, Protarchus is also right in asserting that all are alike in respect of being pleasures. Moreover, although Plato appears to regard pleasure as a generic Form having subordinate species, the difference between a good pleasure and a bad one is very different from that between blue and yellow or circle and square. Socrates does later allow (40D) that any pleasure, for whatever reason it is felt, must be a real pleasure (ἦν μὲν χαίρειν ὄντως ἀεὶ τῷ τὸ παράπαν ὁπωσοῦν καὶ εἰκῇ χαίροντι); but he only concedes this after he has extorted from Protarchus an assent to the legitimacy of assimilating falsity of pleasures to falsity of opinions. Protarchus's case, as put for him by Socrates at 36E, is in fact correct. But Socrates appears to believe that although he concedes that anyone experiences a pleasure who thinks he experiences a pleasure, he has still controverted Protarchus. He summarizes his own conclusion at 42A where he claims to have shown that true and false opinions can 'infect' pleasures and

---

[1] Similarly at *Pol.* 281 A–B Plato speaks of false naming, whereas although names can be inaccurate, or misleading, or wrong, a 'false' name can only be naturally spoken of to mean a pseudonym consciously assumed for the purpose of deception, like a false beard or a false nose.

pains with their truth or falsity (τοῦ παρ' αὐταῖς παθήματος ἀνεπίμπλα-σαν). If Plato meant that we may loosely call pleasures false because a man who anticipates pleasure (and derives pleasure thereby) may be making an erroneous prognostication, then there would not be grounds for impugning Plato's conception of truth and falsity. But as Gosling[1] correctly points out in his analysis of 35 C–41 B, such an interpretation can only be maintained with equanimity at some distance from the text. When Socrates remarks at 37 E 10–11 that pleasure often accompanies false opinion, Protarchus rightly replies that in such cases we call the opinion false, but nobody could ever call the pleasure false. What Plato then represents Protarchus as too readily agreeing to is that this same falsity which attaches to the opinion attaches also to the pleasure.

It will not be necessary to attempt to follow the argument in detail, for it is the conclusion rather than the method by which it is reached that is important for the present discussion. But it is clear that Plato is attempting to vindicate a use of 'false' which cannot be regarded as linguistically proper. This is not to say that to speak of pleasures as true or false is to use these words without meaning, for by speaking of a pleasure as 'true' we may wish to refer (as in the case of 'true love') to its intensity or its duration or its moral content or all three.[2] But such senses are different from that in which judgements and opinions are true, and there is no legitimate analogy to be drawn between them of the kind that Plato wishes to draw. Indeed, Plato's argument at 40B–C explicitly brings in the moral overtones of 'true', and with them a strong reminder of the old equation of virtue and knowledge. The argument seems to be that the virtuous, since they are dear to the gods, will have true opinions and true pleasures inscribed in the book of their minds, whereas the pleasures which the wicked delight in will be bad ones, at least as a rule. Now of course it is perfectly legitimate to speak of good pleasures and bad ones, just as it is legitimate to speak

---

[1] Gosling, p. 45. The difficulties involved in such an interpretation are concisely summarized by Gosling on pp. 45–6. With his general analysis of the trend of the argument I am substantially in agreement, although I believe that the painter is introduced not so much in order to make pictures a transitional analogy between opinions and pleasures as to represent what it is, in a case of prognostication, which the sentence written in the book of the mind describes.

[2] At 51B ff., where types of 'true' pleasures are considered, their truth is explicitly asserted to depend upon their purity (53 B 10–C2 σύμπασα ἡδονὴ σμικρὰ μεγάλης καὶ ὀλίγη πολλῆς, καθαρὰ λύπης, ἡδίων καὶ ἀληθεστέρα καὶ καλλίων γίγνοιτ' ἄν).

of good opinions and bad ones. But bad pleasures are not false pleasures, and bad men are no more likely to hold mistaken opinions than good men are. Plato seems to be assimilating not only pleasure and opinion but also wickedness and falsehood.

After establishing that a present anticipatory pleasure, which must be a genuine pleasure if it is a pleasure at all, can nevertheless be false, Plato goes on to give two further types of false pleasure. Of these the first is one whereby a false estimate is made of the size of a future pleasure, and the second is one in which a man believes himself to be experiencing a pleasure when he is not in fact doing so. The first is clearly very similar to the original type of false pleasure, and raises no further problems of its own. The second, on the other hand, is very different, for it involves a state of affairs in which Plato wishes to say that the subject, although he believes that he is experiencing a pleasure, is not in fact doing so.[1] This contention is in direct contradiction to the view of Protarchus expressed at 36E that no one can think he feels pleasure or pain without actually doing so, and Plato's attempt to counter this view, which is in fact unsuccessful, raises important issues of its own. These, however, are outside the scope of the present discussion, for they throw no further light on Plato's conception of truth and falsehood. From the preceding argument, the conclusion which we are bound to draw is that Plato's analysis of statement and false statement in the *Sophist* did not lead him to the conclusion that falsehood and truth are logically propositional.

We must be further warned from attributing too much sophistication to Plato on the strength of the *Sophist* by his retention in the *Philebus* of a belief that existence (and therefore, which is more important for our present purpose, knowledge) can be a question of degree. Reference has already been made to the evidence for Plato's continued belief in a degrees-of-reality theory. This has curious consequences when applied to the question of what we know and how we know it, for Plato seems to believe that two cows are somehow less really two than the two with which the philosopher deals, and therefore that although

---

[1] Gosling (p. 44) appears to consider both the last two types of pleasure as similar to each other and quite distinct from the original one. Hackforth, however, points out correctly (Hackforth (1), p. 81) that the final case is importantly different from the other two. He is also right in pointing out that Plato is guilty of a logical howler in attempting to describe as a false pleasure something which on his own argument is false because it is not a pleasure at all.

we may know that two cows and two cows make four cows, this knowledge is somehow less true than the knowledge that two and two make four. The passage in which the philosopher's arithmetic is discussed is of course chiefly notorious as the best evidence which there is within the Platonic dialogues for Plato's belief in arithmetical intermediates.[1] But its importance for our present purpose is its relevance to its context. Plato is arguing that some kinds of knowledge are purer and truer and more precise than others, and it is as an example to illustrate this point that he cites the difference between ordinary and philosophical arithmetic. Whatever view we may believe Plato to have held about the things that the philosopher adds together when he does his sums, he appears to believe that the arithmetical truths of the philosopher are truer truths than the arithmetical truths of the ordinary man. He never recants his belief that that X knows p entails p; but he does seem also to believe that some truths are truer than others. This, of course, is absurd, for it is no less true that two cows and two cows make four cows than that $2+2=4$ or two mathematical units and two mathematical units make four mathematical units. But the *Philebus* makes it difficult to maintain that Plato did not continue to believe that two cows are less perfectly two than what the mathematician counts with because cows are less ontologically respectable. Thus knowledge, even propositional knowledge, varies in degree according to the existential status of the subject of the proposition. In the *Philebus* Plato appears willing to grant that we can know that two cows and two cows make four cows, just as he was prepared to grant in the *Theaetetus* that an eye-witness may have knowledge of the crime that he has seen committed. But, as in the *Theaetetus*, the truest knowledge is knowledge of (or about) the most supremely existent things.[2]

Thus even if we should date the *Timaeus* among the dialogues of the middle period, the *Philebus* tells against those interpreters who find in the *Sophist* a conscious sophistication such as must entail a radical re-

---

[1] *Phil.* 56D–57A. A concise and interesting discussion of the problem of the intermediates has recently been given by Wedberg; but his conclusions cannot be regarded as proved and the whole question must continue to remain disputed.

[2] Cf. 58A4–5 ἀληθεστάτην γνῶσιν, 59A11–B1 τῇ ἀκριβεστάτῃ ἀληθείᾳ, 59B7–8 ἐπιστήμη ...τὸ ἀληθέστατον ἔχουσα and particularly 61D10–E4. All these passages serve to show that Plato is contrasting two types of knowledge, not knowledge and opinion, although he speaks at 58E–59A of most arts and their practitioners as using first of all opinions (πρῶτον μὲν δόξαις χρῶνται).

vision on Plato's part of his earlier tenets. That the *Sophist* does mark certain important advances is, on the other hand, equally certain; and it must be regarded as more important than the *Theaetetus*, although the *Theaetetus* is hardly less interesting. Indeed, as we have seen, the *Theaetetus* is closer in approach to the *Cratylus* than to the *Sophist*. But the *Sophist* remains interesting as much for what it does not achieve as for what it does, although it marks Plato's successful emancipation from his earlier atomism. The modern reader of the *Sophist* is continually given the feeling that if only Plato had not been mistaken about the nature of his subject-matter, he would have broken through to an astonishingly sophisticated understanding of the structure and function of language. What prevented this break-through it is perhaps not possible to say. But it is at least tempting to ascribe the prevention directly to Plato's dogged retention of the Theory of Forms, despite the criticisms of the *Parmenides* and the different method of approach which succeeded them. If a philosopher can be said to be doing logic without knowing it, then we may say that Plato in the *Sophist* is doing logic. But Cornford, despite his misunderstanding at many points of what it is that Plato is attempting to do, is right to reject Taylor's claim[1] that in the *Sophist* logic is for the first time in the literature of philosophy contemplated as an autonomous science. Plato, of course, is a very great deal closer to it than his predecessors. But it must still be true that the founder of logic is not Plato but Aristotle.

[1] Taylor, *op. cit.* p. 387.

IV

CONCLUSION

An attempt has been made in this essay to give a coherent interpretation of the *Theaetetus* and *Sophist* as a whole, and to consider what light they throw on Plato's later attitude to the problems of the nature of knowledge and the nature of truth and error. Such an attempt cannot deal thoroughly with all the detailed problems of interpretation which these dialogues raise, nor can it undertake a systematic rebuttal of the views of others. But I hope to have shown that a reasonable interpretation of the principal arguments can be put forward such that both the *Theaetetus* and *Sophist* may be seen to be saying something newer and more important than such conservative interpreters as Cornford and Cherniss believe, although less new and less important than is maintained by those who find in these dialogues the doctrines and approach of twentieth-century logical analysis. This intermediate position does not require us to impute to Plato a recantation of his earlier doctrines which there is no evidence that he made; but neither does it deny to his arguments a greater relevance to contemporary philosophical problems than is to be found in any other of his dialogues. Accordingly, it only remains to consider the view here put forward in the context of Plato's writings as a whole.

Of the many difficult questions raised by speculation about the early Academy, not the least difficult is why its members seem neither to have been conscious of a development in Plato's ideas, nor to have sought from him directly the resolution of the problems which, then as now, his teaching posed. Thus those who took notes on the Lecture on the Good seem to have disputed among each other as to its meaning; but they turned for arbitration of their differences not to Plato himself, but to such assistance as they could get from isolated passages in the dialogues. Similarly, Aristotle is notorious for his almost unfailing propensity to treat all parts of Plato's teachings as part of a unified and consistent system. But on grounds of simple probability it must be virtually impossible to believe that a philosopher of Plato's originality and power, who lived until the age of eighty and was writing when he died, should not have considerably altered and improved upon his earlier ideas. Indeed, that some development took place is of necessity allowed even by those interpreters who wish to keep any and all such development to a minimum; and it is Aristotle himself who, despite his approach, gives much of the evidence which it is hardest to equate with a unitarian approach to Plato. Thus whatever the answer to the puzzles of the Academy, these puzzles cannot be used against a probability to which the dialogues themselves, on any dating now held, must be regarded as giving support. No further justification, in my opinion, is needed for accepting a view that Plato's ideas must have undergone considerable and important modification during the course of his life and writings;[1] and it is with this assumption in mind that the *Theaetetus* and *Sophist* may be best understood.

The most striking feature of the later dialogues, as commentators have frequently pointed out, is not so much a difference of doctrine, although this is discernible, as of approach. To this general trend the *Timaeus* stands out as something of an exception (although we are not thereby necessarily obliged to assign it to the middle period). But the later dialogues are on the whole more modest in aim and more analytical in tone than the *Phaedo, Symposium* and *Republic*. In this development, it is the *Parmenides* which marks the watershed. Plato, in the *Parmenides*, although he reaffirms his belief that without the Forms meaningful discourse would be impossible, still undertakes a serious and penetrating criticism of his own theory; and it is by the method of Division first expounded in the *Phaedrus*, not the method of Hypothesis, that he subsequently undertakes his exposition of the Forms. This new method does not only cover the dichotomous classification of genera into species, for it includes also the demarcation of the μέγιστα γένη of the *Sophist* and the account which is given of their interrelations. But the predominant difference which the new method embodies is that the Forms are no longer seen as the isolated objects of hypothesis and deduction so much as members of a complicated structure of mutual interrelations. It is these relations and the rules (or, to Plato, properties of certain particular Forms) that govern them which are explicitly pronounced to be the task of the dialectician.

More or less concurrent with the development of the method of

---

[1] Cf. E. R. Dodds, *The Greeks and the Irrational* (University of California, 1951), pp. 208–9.

Division is Plato's preoccupation with letters and syllables. These are first discussed in the *Cratylus*, and reappear in the *Phaedrus*. They are then either discussed or used as an analogy in the *Theaetetus*, *Sophist*, *Politicus* and *Philebus*, as well as (very briefly) in the *Timaeus* (48 B 7– C 2). In the *Sophist*, as we have seen, Plato uses the analogy of letters to illustrate the connecting functions of certain pervasive 'vowel' Forms. In the *Politicus*, however, where the analogy is used without such immediate relevance to the world of Forms, it throws an interesting light on the change in Plato's view from even the time of the *Theaetetus*. The Eleatic stranger gives as an example of an example the case of children learning how to spell (277 C–278 C). He points out that they are first taught how to recognize individual letters in simple combinations and then in progressively more difficult ones. The implication of this is that they cannot be said really to know their letters until they know how they combine with other letters; and this is clearly a different point of view from that of the *Theaetetus*, in which it was asserted that knowledge of letters and notes must be prior to and independent of knowledge of syllables and tunes. This does not mean that Plato recanted the conclusion of the *Theaetetus* that knowledge cannot be only of complexes, for we have seen that there is no evidence that he did so; and the *Politicus* analogy does not entail that letters are knowable only in syllables. Plato never wishes to say, as Frege does, that only in the context of a sentence does a name stand for anything. But the analogy serves to show how much more importance Plato had come to attach to the rules of combination and interrelation between simples. He appears to continue to believe that the philosopher has intuitive knowledge by acquaintance of the Forms. But the change since the middle dialogues is that knowledge of certain Forms involves knowledge of the connecting properties which they possess, and the philosopher is now concerned less with contemplation than correlation.

This question is a different one from that of how far the later dialogues modify the separation of particulars from Forms. It is in any case debatable just how radical this separation ever was; but the nature of the relation between particulars and Forms is a problem to which Plato never gives a satisfactory or even an explicit solution, and neither the *Theaetetus* nor the *Sophist* is of any great help in the attempt to find one. The problem appears to be touched upon at the beginning of the *Philebus*, but it is not effectively followed up; and indeed in the

Timaeus Plato goes so far as to say at 68 D that only God can combine many into one and dissolve one into many, although this may not have reference to more than the discussion of colour which provides its context. That Plato retained the Theory of Forms after writing the *Parmenides* is evident, and we can only conclude that he believed that the difficulty of describing the relation of particulars to Forms should not be regarded as fatal to the theory. His misplaced confidence may perhaps have been strengthened by what we have seen to be his persistent assimilation of Forms to their extensions. Throughout the later dialogues, the reader (and perhaps, therefore, Plato) is confused as to just what is being talked about. No unambiguous distinction is made between Sophistry and a sophist, Difference and what is different, Whiteness and white, Pleasure and a pleasure. What degree of conscious or unconscious confusion should be attributed to Plato it is very difficult to say, although it is hard to share Cornford's conviction that Plato employs deliberate and conscious ambiguities which the trained Academic reader is supposed to detect. But Plato appears never to have arrived at any satisfactory logical disentanglement of particulars and Forms or to have worked out any coherent account of their relation.

This is not to say that the Theory of Forms as we find it in the later dialogues is not very different from the Theory of Forms as expounded in the *Phaedo* and *Republic*. Indeed, in the *Philebus* the Forms are even referred to by the words 'monad' and 'henad' which are used of them nowhere else. But it is still a Theory of Forms; that is to say, a theory of suprasensible entities whose existence must be the necessary prerequisite of all thought and speech. It is true that the Forms do not feature very prominently in the late dialogues. They are almost totally irrelevant to the *Laws* and scarcely less so to most of the *Theaetetus*. It is now generally agreed that they do not feature in the notorious tetrachotomy of the *Philebus*, and it is only in that Statesmanship is a Form that they are really relevant to the *Politicus*. In the *Timaeus*, if late, they play an important part, but even in the *Sophist* it is only certain very special Forms that are under discussion. However, the Forms are still unmistakably there, even in the *Laws*, where there is in the final book a brief but unmistakable reference to them; and it is precisely because they are still there that Plato is prevented from talking about propositions or classes or even language as such. Only Aristotle, after his total emancipation from the Forms, was able to do what Plato seems just about to do all through the *Sophist*. But Plato's retention of the Forms meant that for him all questions must remain questions of ontology.

On the other hand, we are not bound to follow Robinson's austere canons of interpretation[1] and argue that because Plato had no word for 'ambiguity' or 'copula' he must necessarily have had no consciousness of ambiguity and have failed to discover the copula. It is quite true that he nowhere gives an analysis of ambiguity such as was later carried out by Aristotle; and, as I have tried to show, the claim that he discovered the copula cannot be accepted without modification. But he does show some consciousness of ambiguity, if only by the phrase οὐχ ὁμοίως εἰρήκαμεν, and his awareness of the different uses of εἶναι could well have led him to an explicit differentiation of the copulative sense as such. Plato, in fact, is doing some very sophisticated philosophy under some very ingenious self-imposed handicaps. Although still shackled by the limitations of the Theory of Forms, he contrives in the *Theaetetus* and *Sophist* to say things both interesting and useful on such important philosophical problems as ostension and identity, change, error, meaning and statement, existence, negation, and sense-data. The fact that Plato did not formulate these problems as subsequent philosophers have been able to formulate them does not make it illegitimate to claim that these problems were what he was talking about; and in the *Theaetetus* and *Sophist* he says something about each of them which he had not said in any previous dialogue.

The *Theaetetus* must be regarded as the less important of the two, for although it achieves its ostensible purpose of giving grounds for rejecting the equation of knowledge with either perception or true opinion or true opinion plus logos, it fails to answer the question of what knowledge really is, and fails also to resolve the problem of error which occupies its central section. Its most interesting part is Socrates' 'dream', as is testified by the amount of recent literature in which it is discussed and by the parallel drawn by Wittgenstein himself between it and the logical atomism of the earlier Wittgenstein and Russell. But its most important part from the point of view of the actual development of Plato's thought is the treatment of flux in the earlier section of the dialogue, which is followed up by the arguments on Change in the *Sophist*. It is doubtful, however, whether the *Sophist* should be regarded

[1] Robinson (3), pp. 1–6.

as the predetermined sequel to the *Theaetetus*. Although it is dramatically presented to be a resumed conversation which takes place on the morning after the conversation reported in the *Theaetetus*, the stylometric evidence suggests that some time may have elapsed between the composition of the two. The affinities of the *Theaetetus* are with the *Parmenides* and *Phaedrus*, while the affinities of the *Sophist* are with the *Politicus* and *Philebus*; and it is not improbable, though it cannot be at all certain, that the *Theaetetus* was composed before, and the *Sophist* after, Plato's second visit to the court of Dionysius. Moreover, although Plato's aporetic conclusions may be deceptive (as in the *Meno*), and although more than one dialogue may deal with the same philosophical problem, it does not seem to be Plato's habit deliberately to set problems in one dialogue which are to be solved in another. The *Sophist* does make possible a resolution of the problems of error which are expounded in the *Theaetetus*. But it does not directly answer them, and it is concerned with the problems of statement and false statement rather than with the problems of knowledge and erroneous judgement.

It is possible, with Ross,[1] to regard the *Theaetetus* as giving Plato's fullest statement of the grounds on which his metaphysical theory rests, for it does in fact embody his most detailed attack on the equation of knowledge with perception or opinion, and the arguments against Protagoras and Heraclitus (as Plato chooses to understand them) are, although not stated as such, at least as good arguments for the Forms as those in the *Phaedo* and the central section of the *Republic*. But the *Theaetetus* gives neither an exposition of the Theory of Forms nor of the nature of philosophical knowledge and only in its treatment of the sensible world marks an important advance from Plato's earlier position. It is the *Sophist* which is the most novel as well as the most sophisticated of all Plato's dialogues, for the *Philebus*, important and difficult though it is, is in many ways something of a reversion to Pythagoreanism. Plato's later dialectical method achieves in the *Sophist* its most significant and interesting results. Indeed, it achieves these results when it is least concerned with the dichotomous classification according to genus and species in which the whole of the *Sophist* is ostensibly an exercise. The limitations of the method prevent Plato, as they did not, of course, prevent Aristotle, from distinguishing the formal from the contentual features of propositions. Plato never

[1] Ross, p. 103.

evolved any code-symbolism in which the formal features could be manipulated and analysed. But he realized that the properties and relations of his μέγιστα γένη were different in kind from, as well as more pervasive than, the Forms which stand for concepts which can be classified under genus and species. Thus Ryle is right to point out that Plato avoids the logical embarrassments into which Meinong's courageous but unfortunate pertinacity was to lead him, for Plato's Being and non-Being are not, as Meinong's existence and non-existence are, co-ordinate species of a generic concept. It is this realization by Plato which makes the analysis of the μέγιστα γένη perhaps the most ingenious and important passage in the whole of his dialogues.

There is, of course, a whole other line of development in Plato's writings which this discussion has altogether ignored, namely the course of his political views which must be traced from the *Republic* through the *Politicus* to the *Laws*. I do not wish, by emphasizing the importance of the *Sophist*, to be thought to belittle in any way the importance of Plato's doctrines of politics and government. But my concern has been with Plato's treatment of topics in the philosophy of language rather than ethics or politics, although I am well aware that Plato himself made no such clear-cut distinctions as those which dictate the demarcation of my particular interests within his work as a whole. What I have tried to show is that in the *Theaetetus* and *Sophist*, although both are written within the framework of the brilliant but misguided Theory of Forms, Plato says new and interesting things which are still relevant to philosophy as we now understand it. This does not make him the first of the school of logical analysis, nor does it make him the repetitious propagandist of the unitarian interpreters. But that he was able in the later period of his work to propound new and important philosophical discoveries, although still bound within the terms of his own original theory, is a measure of his real greatness as a philosopher.

SELECTED BIBLIOGRAPHY

ACKRILL, J. L. (1). 'ΣΥΜΠΛΟΚΗ ΕΙΔΩΝ', *Bulletin of the Institute of Classical Studies in the University of London*, No. 2 (1955), pp. 31–5.

—— (2). 'Plato and the Copula: *Sophist* 251–259', *Journal of Hellenic Studies* LXXVII (1957 (1)), pp. 1–6.

ALLAN, D. J. 'The Problem of Cratylus', *American Journal of Philology* LXXV (1954), pp. 271–87.

BLUCK, R. S. (1). *Plato's Phaedo* (London, 1955).

—— (2). 'Logos and Forms in Plato: a Reply to Professor Cross', *Mind*, n.s. LXV (1956), pp. 522–9.

—— (3). 'False Statement in the *Sophist*', *Journal of Hellenic Studies* LXXVII (1957 (2)), pp. 181–6.

—— (4). 'Forms as Standards', *Phronesis* II (1957), pp. 115–27.

CAMPBELL, L. (1). *The Sophist and Statesman of Plato* (Oxford, 1867).

—— (2). *The Theaetetus of Plato*² (Oxford, 1883).

CHERNISS, H. F. (1). 'The Philosophical Economy of the Theory of Ideas', *American Journal of Philology* LVII (1936), pp. 445–56.

—— (2). *Aristotle's Criticism of Plato and the Academy*, vol. 1 (Baltimore, 1944).

—— (3). *The Riddle of the Early Academy* (University of California, 1945).

—— (4). 'A Much Misread Passage of the *Timaeus* (*Timaeus* 49 C 7–50 B 5)', *American Journal of Philology* LXXV (1954), pp. 113–30.

—— (5). '*Timaeus* 38 A 8–B 5', *Journal of Hellenic Studies* LXXVII (1957 (1)), pp. 18–23.

—— (6). 'The Relation of the *Timaeus* to Plato's Later Dialogues', *American Journal of Philology* LXXVIII (1957), pp. 225–66.

CORNFORD, F. M. *Plato's Theory of Knowledge* (London, 1935).

CROSS, R. C. 'Logos and Forms in Plato', *Mind*, n.s. LXIII (1954), pp. 433–50.

DÜRR, K. 'Die Moderne Darstellung der Platonischen Logik', *Museum Helveticum* II (1945), pp. 166–94.

GOLDSCHMIDT, V. *Essai sur le Cratyle* (Paris, 1940).

GOSLING, J. 'False Pleasures: *Philebus* 35 c–41 b', *Phronesis* IV (1959), pp. 44–53.

GOULD, J. *The Development of Plato's Ethics* (Cambridge, 1955).

HACKFORTH, R. (1). *Plato's Examination of Pleasure* (Cambridge, 1945).

—— (2). 'False Statement in Plato's *Sophist*', *Classical Quarterly* XXXIX (1945), pp. 56–8.

—— (3). *Plato's Phaedrus* (Cambridge, 1952).

—— (4). 'Platonic Forms in the *Theaetetus*', *Classical Quarterly*, n.s. VII (1957), pp. 53–8.

HAMLYN, D. W. (1). 'The Communion of the Forms and the Development of Plato's Logic', *Philosophical Quarterly* V (1955), pp. 289–302.

—— (2). 'Forms and Knowledge in Plato's *Theaetetus*: a Reply to Mr Bluck', *Mind*, n.s. LXVI (1957), p. 547.

HARDIE, W. F. R. *A Study in Plato* (Oxford, 1936).

HICKEN, WINIFRED (1). 'Knowledge and Forms in Plato's *Theaetetus*', *Journal of Hellenic Studies* LXXVII (1957 (1)), pp. 48–53.

—— (2). 'The Character and Provenance of Socrates' Dream in the *Theaetetus*', *Phronesis* III (1958), pp. 126–45.

ISENBERG, M. W. 'Plato's *Sophist* and the Five Stages of Knowing', *Classical Philology* XLVI (1951), pp. 201–11.

JAEGER, W. *Aristotle* (tr. R. Robinson, Oxford, 1934).

KIRK, G. S. 'The Problem of Cratylus', *American Journal of Philology* LXXII (1951), pp. 225–53.

KOHNKE, F. W. 'Plato's Conception of τὸ οὐκ ὄντως οὐκ ὄν', *Phronensis* II (1957), pp. 32–40.

LEVINSON, R. B. 'Language and the *Cratylus*: Four Questions', *Review of Metaphysics* XI (1957), pp. 28–41.

LUTOSLAWSKI, W. *The Origin and Growth of Plato's Logic* (London, 1897).

MEYERHOFF, H. 'Socrates' "Dream" in the *Theaetetus*', *Classical Quarterly*, n.s. VIII (1958), pp. 131–8.

MORAVCSIK, J. M. E. 'Mr Xenakis on Truth and Meaning', *Mind*, n.s. LXVII (1958), pp. 533–7.

NAKHNIKIAN, G. 'Plato's Theory of Sensation', *Review of Metaphysics* IX (1955), pp. 129–48, 306–27.

OWEN, G. E. L. (1). 'The Place of the *Timaeus* in Plato's Dialogues', *Classical Quarterly*, n.s. III (1953), pp. 79–95.

—— (2). 'A Proof in the ΠΕΡΙ ΙΔΕѠΝ', *Journal of Hellenic Studies* LXXVII (1957 (1)), pp. 103–11.

PARAIN, B. *Essai sur le Logos Platonicien* (Paris, 1942).

PECK, A. L. 'Plato and the ΜΕΓΙΣΤΑ ΓΕΝΗ of the *Sophist*: a Reinterpretation', *Classical Quarterly*, n.s. II (1952), pp. 32–56.

ROBINSON, R. (1). 'Plato's Consciousness of Fallacy', *Mind*, n.s. LI (1942), pp. 97–114.

—— (2). 'Forms and Error in Plato's *Theaetetus*', *Philosophical Review* LIX (1950), pp. 3–30.

—— (3). *Plato's Earlier Dialectic*[2] (Oxford, 1953).

—— (4). 'A Criticism of Plato's *Cratylus*', *Philosophical Review* LXV (1956), pp. 324–41.

ROSS, W. D. *Plato's Theory of Ideas*[2] (Oxford, 1953).

RYLE, G. 'Plato's *Parmenides*', *Mind*, n.s. XLVIII (1939), pp. 129–51, 302–25, esp. pp. 317–25.

SKEMP, J. *Plato's Statesman* (London, 1952).

STENZEL, J. *Plato's Method of Dialectic* (tr. D. J. Allan, Oxford, 1940).

VLASTOS, G. 'Socratic Knowledge and Platonic Pessimism', *Philosophical Review* LXVI (1957), pp. 226–38.

WEDBERG, A. *Plato's Philosophy of Mathematics* (Stockholm, 1955).

XENAKIS, J. 'Plato on Statement and Truth-Value', *Mind*, n.s. LXVI (1957), pp. 165–72.

YOLTON, J. W. 'The Ontological Status of Sense-Data in Plato's Theory of Perception', *Review of Metaphysics* III (1949), pp. 21–58.

INDEX

Academy, 56 n., 60 n., 63 n., 76, 91 n.,
  103, 127–8
Ackrill, J. L., 63 n., 83 n., 84 n., 85, 88, 89 n.,
  90, 104 n., 108 n.
αἰτίας λογισμός, 8–9
Alexander of Aphrodisias, 11 n., 60 n.,
  65–6, 103
Allan, D. J., 2 n., 17 n.
anamnesis, 9, 21
Antisthenes, 18 n., 94 n.
Aristippus, 19
Aristophanes, 34 n.
Aristotle, 20 n., 21, 23, 56, 65–6, 91 n.,
  94 n., 110, 126–32 passim
  An. Pr., 11 n., 47 n.
  Cat., 10 n.
  De An., 10 n.
  De Gen. et Corr., 56 n., 81
  De Int., 21 n., 33 n., 109
  De Part An., 56 n.
  Eth. Nic., 12, 43 n.
  Met., 17 n., 18 n., 20 n., 47, 50 n., 53 n.
  Phys., 17 n., 99 n.
Aristoxenus, 56 n.
von Arnim, H., 2, 3
Ayer, A. J., 38 n.

Bluck, R. S., 8 n., 10 n., 54 n., 75 n., 108 n.,
  111 n., 114 n.
Brumbaugh, Robert S., 11 n.
Burnet, J., 19, 25 n., 68, 115 n.

Campbell, L., 17 n., 19, 68, 76 n.
Carnap, R., 62 n.
Cherniss, H. F., 2 n., 4, 17 n., 18 n., 56 n.,
  63 n., 76 n., 78 n., 127
copula, 63, 76, 84, 88 ff., 97–8, 104, 105–6,
  131
Cornford, F. M., passim
Cratylus, 17 n., 20 n.
Cross, R. C., 8 n., 10 n.

Denniston, J. D., 42
Diels, H., 27 n.
Diès, A., 53 n., 68
Diogenes Laertius, 3 n., 18 n., 65 n., 91 n.,
  94 n.

Dionysius of Halicarnassus, 3 n.
division (diaeresis), 5, 56 n., 58, 59 ff., 120,
  128
Dodds, E. R., 128 n.
δόξα, δοξάζειν, 6 n., 10 n., 14, 16, 27 n., 29,
  30, 33, 34, 35, 42, 48, 125 n.
δύναμις, 23 n., 48 n., 77 n., 81, 82, 93
Dürr, K., 89 n., 108 n.

εἰδέναι, 16, 34, 37, 43 n.
Empedocles, 44
Epicharmus, 13 n.
Epicrates, 63 n.
ἐπιστήμη (ἐπίστασθαι, ἐπιστητός), 10 ff., 23,
  34, 35, 39, 43, 125 n.
error, 30 ff., 45, 52, 113, 119–20, 131, 132
Eudoxus, 4

flux, 6, 13, 14, 17 ff., 29, 75, 79, 81, 131
Forms, 8 n., 18, 19, 20 ff., 34, 37, 38 n., 54 ff.,
  60 n., 61, 62, 76 ff., 84 ff., 100 ff.,
  116 ff., 121, 122, 126, 128 ff.
Frege, G., 32 n., 36, 129

γένεσις, 4, 22, 23 n., 76–7, 78 n.
γνῶναι, γνῶσις, 27, 35, 43 n., 125 n.
Goldschmidt, V., 2 n., 18 n.
Gosling, J., 123, 124 n.
Gould, J., 4 n., 12 n., 55 n.
Grote, G., 21 n.

Hackforth, R., 3, 10, 19 n., 36 n., 108 n.,
  124 n.
Hamlyn, D. W., 8 n., 43 n., 62 n., 108 n.
Heath, Sir T. L., 11 n.
Heraclitus, Heracliteans, 6, 13, 17, 20 n., 132
Hermodorus, 91 n.
Hicken, Winifred, 8, 9 n., 43 n.
Homer, 13 n.

Jackson, H., 19

κίνησις, 17, 23 n., 72, 75 n., 80, 81, 83, 88,
  89, 92, 93, 97
Kirk, G. S., 2 n., 17 n., 30 n.
Kohnke, F. W., 68 n.
κομψοί, 18–19

Leonard, H. S., 66 n.
logos, 6, 7, 8–9, 16 n., 32 ff., 55, 56, 84, 106–7, 109–10, 116
Lutoslawski, W., 10 n., 77 n.

μέγιστα γένη, 58, 61, 62, 83 ff., 104, 107, 116, 128, 133
memory, 14, 36
μετέχειν (μέθεξις), 88, 89–91, 95 n., 97–8, 104–6, 112
Meyerhoff, H., 44 n.
Moravcsik, J. M. E., 61 n., 108 n.

Nakhnikian, G., 75 n.
names, naming, 20–1, 32–3, 43, 51, 54, 60, 73–4, 86–7
νόμος, 21 n., 60

ὀνόματα (see also names), 32, 33, 39 ff., 55, 94 n., 107 n., 108 n.
οὐσία, 4, 15, 22, 23 n., 55, 74, 76–7, 78 n.
Owen, G. E. L., 2 n., 4, 18 n., 20, 78 n., 91 n.

Parmenides, 17, 59, 70, 82, 99
Peck, A. L., 108 n.
Plato, passim. Order of dialogues, 1–4
  Charm., 10 n., 12, 31 n., 42, 55 n., 116 n.
  Crat., 2, 12, 17 n., 20–1, 25, 31, 32–3, 36 n., 54, 57, 60, 76 n., 79, 114, 119, 126, 129
  Ep. VII, 53, 54, 57
  Ep. XI, 53 n.
  Ep. XIII, 56 n.
  Euthyd., 11, 31, 57
  Gorg., 9 n., 19 n., 78, 110 n.
  Hipp. Ma., 19 n.
  Laches, 12, 49 n.
  Laws, 4, 21 n., 23, 27, 54–5, 56, 75, 78 n., 80, 81, 130
  Lecture on the Good, 56, 127
  Lysis, 19 n., 78
  Meno, 7, 8–9, 21, 31 n., 49 n., 116 n., 132, 133
  Parm., 1, 3, 4, 7, 18, 21, 23, 26, 27 n., 38, 57 n., 58, 77 n., 80, 82, 91 n., 102 n., 126, 128, 130, 132
  Phaed., 2, 3, 8 n., 9 n., 22, 25, 26, 42, 58, 76 n., 78, 81, 103, 128, 130, 132
  Phaedr., 2, 10 n., 23, 28, 38, 48 n., 53, 63, 128, 129, 132
  Phil., 2, 13 n., 17, 19, 22, 23, 34, 36–7, 38, 45, 48, 54, 56, 57 n., 61 n., 63, 69 n., 80, 119, 120, 121, 122 ff., 129, 130, 132

'Philosopher', 53–4
  Pol., 1, 4, 13 n., 19, 21 n., 48, 53, 55 n., 60, 61 n., 103, 122 n., 129, 132, 133
  Prot., 11, 49 n., 73 n., 110
  Rep., 2, 9, 10 n., 12, 13 n., 21 n., 22, 23, 25, 26, 27, 28, 40, 49 n., 52, 65, 66, 128, 130, 132, 133
  Soph., 59–126 et passim
  Symp., 2, 3, 9 n., 33 n., 128
  Theaet., 6–58 et passim
  Tim., 3, 4, 9 n., 22, 44, 56, 61 n., 69 n., 75, 80 n., 125, 128, 129, 130
Plutarch, 108 n.
Pohlenz, M., 2 n.
Protagoras, 6, 13, 26
Pythagoreans, 19 n.

Quine, W. V., 64, 65, 66 n., 79

ῥῆμα, 25, 33 n., 108 n.
Rescher, N., 66 n.
Ritter, C., 3, 77 n.
Robinson, R., 8, 9, 10, 17 n., 20, 30, 38, 46 n., 73 n., 108 n., 131
Ross, Sir W. D., 2 n., 11 n., 18, 56 n., 76 n., 78, 108 n., 132
Ryle, G., 12, 133

self-predication, 75 n., 80, 90, 95, 97, 101–2
sense-data, 19–20, 24–5
Sextus Empiricus, 30 n., 91 n.
Simplicius, 4 n., 56 n., 91 n.
Skemp, J., 19 n., 53
Socrates' 'dream', 5, 7, 33 n., 39 ff., 64 n., 94 n., 108 n., 131
Stenzel, J., 61
στοιχεῖα, 41, 44
Strawson, P. F., 32 n., 33 n.
συμπλοκή, 39, 45, 46, 108, 109, 111–13
syllables, 44, 45–6, 47–8, 50, 94 n., 129

Taylor, A. E., 55 n., 77 n., 126
truth-value, 1, 36–7, 120 ff.

Vlastos, G., 4 n., 12 n., 17 n., 55 n.

Warburg, M., 2
Wasserstein, A., 11 n.
Wedberg, A., 125 n.
Wittgenstein, L., 32 n., 46, 100 n., 131

φύσις, 21 n., 48 n., 60, 95 n., 102

χωρισμός, 26, 76 n.